GOD'S HEALTH CARE PLAN

Chuck Schiappacasse

Unless otherwise indicated, all scriptures are taken from the NEW AMERICAN STANDARD BIBLE, c 1960, 1962, 1963, 1968, 1971, 1972, 1973, 1975, 1977, by the Lockman Foundation. Used by permission. The following standard abbreviations are indicated when other versions are quoted: KJV for the King James Version, NKJV for the New King James Version and NIV for the New International Version.

CONTENTS

CONTENTS

About the Author

Chuck Schiappacasse is a free-lance marketing writer. Along with his wife, Faye, he's on the volunteer staff of Good News Church in Des Plaines, Illinois. Chuck and Faye head nursing home and door-to-door outreach ministries of the church.

In their more than a dozen years of ministry, the Schiappacasses have been involved in a growing number of healings and deliverances. A large percentage of the cases noted in this book have been taken from their experiences.

Chuck's previous book, "God Heals Today", which features over 70 medically-confirmed cases of divine healing, is available in many bookstores and can also be ordered by calling **1-800-760-BOOK.**

FOREWORD

Health care.

It's essential for untold millions. The cost is climbing to untold billions.

But can anyone possibly provide the comprehensive coverage and curative care we need at a price we can live with? Wouldn't it be wonderful if such a plan existed?

Well, it does. And wonderful may be the best way to describe it.

The truth is, you and I can take advantage of the most universal, comprehensive and inexpensive health care plan ever created.

And where can we find out about such a plan? In the Bible. It's all there, chapter and verse.

God has provided it, yet very few people, including most Christians (who are automatically enrolled) are even aware of it.

If you have ever been involved with sickness, pain, fear, anxiety, depression or any other physical, mental or emotional affliction, you should know the mind-boggling benefits of God's unique health insurance.

This unparalleled divine plan is in place and available right now. To find out about God's heavenly health care program, including His HMO (Health Maintenance Organization), just read on. What you discover could revolutionize your life!

Know Your Carrier

It's always good business to know whom you're dealing with. Especially in health care. What about the source? Is it reliable? Does it have what it takes? Has it been around for a while? Is the provider cold and remote or warm and accessible? Is it responsive to your need? Are promises likely to be kept? What about the cost? Does your source believe in full disclosure? Since such considerations are important, here are a few facts you should know about the Divine Provider.

His Nature: "God is love." *(I John 5:8)*

His Longevity: "You are from everlasting to everlasting" *(Psalm 93: 5 NKJV)*

His Faithfulness: "I am with you always" *(Matthew 28:20)*

His Willingness: "And moved with compassion, He stretched out His hand and touched him, and said to him, "I am willing; be cleansed." *(Mark 1:40)*

His Generosity: "Every good thing bestowed and every perfect gift is from above" *(James 1:17)*

His Open-Handedness: "He Who did not spare His own Son, but delivered Him up for us all, how will He not also with Him freely give us all things?" *(Romans 8:32)*

His Financial Condition: "The silver is Mine, and the gold is Mine" *(Haggai 2:8)*

His Truthfulness: "God is not a man, that He should lie" *(Numbers 23:19)*

His Capability: "Behold, I am the Lord, the God of all flesh. Is anything too difficult for Me?" *(Jeremiah 32:27)*

His Love: "His loving kindness is everlasting" *(Psalm 118:29)*

His Responsiveness: "Call to Me and I will answer you" *(Jeremiah 33:3)*

His Dedication to Good Health: "I wish above all things that thou mayest prosper and be in health" *(III John 2 KJV)*

His Compassion: "The Lord is gracious and merciful" *(Psalm 145:8)*

His Authority: "All authority has been given to Me in heaven and on earth." *(Matthew 28:20)*

His Healing Credentials: "He cast out the spirits with a word and healed all who were ill." *(Matthew 8:16)*

His Power: "You have made the heavens and the earth by your great power." *(Jeremiah 32:17 NKJV)*

His Total Care: "And my God shall supply all your needs" *(Phillipians 4:19)*

His Rating: **AAAAAAAAAAAMEN**

What other health care provider can possibly rate as high?

Check the Record

"I would above things that thou mayest ..be in health"
(III John 2 KJV)

God wants His people healthy - and He backs His word on it. After he pulled over three million individuals out of Egypt - and there wasn't one feeble among them *(Psalm 105:7)* - He revealed Himself to Moses as "the Lord Who heals you." *(Exodus 15:26 NKJV)*

History records that for hundreds of years, doctors were not necessary for Israel. God was it. It wasn't until King Solomon made a politically-correct marriage with Pharaoh's daughter that the medical practices of Egypt came into Israel. Even then, God preferred His people to come to Him for healing. When they did, He came through.

When the son of a widow of Sidon died, God used the prophet Elijah to stretch out over the boy and sent His healing power through the prophet to raise the boy from the dead. *(I Kings 17:21,22)* That's healing about as hopeless a health problem as you're likely to encounter.

God is for life. After all, His Son came to give us a more abundant life. *(John 10:10)* And to prove it, the literal Hebrew translation of Isaiah 53:4,5 prophesies that the Messiah (Jesus) would bear our sicknesses and pains and by the scourging He bore, we ARE healed. Matthew 8:16 records that Jesus fulfilled that prophecy by healing EVERYONE who came to Him. Then, before His crucifixion, Jesus, God in the flesh, did bear every sickness and pain on Himself when He was scourged, paying the price for all healing. Now, that's about committed to health care as you can get.

In the New Testament, the apostle Peter looks back at the cross and states that by Jesus' scourging we were healed. (I Peter 2:24) And, of course, during His entire ministry, Jesus went around healing multitudes and never turned anyone away.

In the Acts of the Apostles (after Jesus' resurrection), God kept healing people through His apostles and disciples as they used the name of Jesus.

In Acts 5:16, everyone who poured into the city was healed. Acts

27:9 records that God healed everyone who was sick on the island of Malta.

God also wants to heal every part of everyone. In First Thessalonians 5:23, we discover the words "May your whole spirit, soul and body be preserved complete."

Today, God continues to fulfill His healing promises all over the world.

In "God Heals Today," we report over 70 medically-confirmed cases of divine healing in the Chicago area alone. As you read on in this book, you'll find more stories of healing - this time, mental and emotional, as well as physical.

Consider God the original promise-keeper manifestly committed to healing.

And since Acts 10:34 reveals that God doesn't show partiality, there are no exclusions to His total health care. You can be included.

Just as God can stand on His proof of performance, so can you!

Here are yet a few more promises and fulfillments from the Promise Keeper

* "He sent His word and healed them" *(Psalm 107:20)*
* "I will restore you to health and I will heal you of your wounds". *(Jeremiah 30:17)*
* "The Sun of Righteousness shall arise with healing in His wings". *(Malachi 4:2 NKJV)*
* "He has sent Me to proclaim release to the captives, and recovery of sight to the blind" *(Luke 4:18)*
* "And standing over her, He rebuked the fever, and it left her". *(Luke 4:39)*
* "And immediately he regained his sight and began following Him on the road" *(Mark 10:52)*
* "..healing every kind of disease and every kind of sickness". *(Matthew 9:35)*
* "And a great multitude was following Him, because they were seeing the signs which He was performing on those who were sick". *(John 6:2)*
* "Jesus Christ is the same yesterday and today, yes and forever". *(Hebrews 13:8)*

* "For as many as may be the promises of God, in Him they are yes" *(II Corinthians 1:20)*

See Your Real Enemy

*"Your adversary, the devil, prowls about like a
roaring lion, seeking someone to devour."*

(I Peter 5:8)

Health care is necessary because there's someone out there to, as Jesus Christ put it, "steal, kill and destroy" *(John 10:10).* That's the devil, or Satan.

The word of God also tells us that Jesus Christ went around healing everyone who was oppressed by the devil. *(Acts 10:38)*

But, why does God allow the devil and his army of evil spirits to sicken, sadden and stress out mankind? Because the devil is "the god of this world", (II *Corinthians 4:4)* and we live in this world.

How in the world did the prince of evil become the ruler of this world? When Adam and Eve fell in the garden of Eden nearly six thousand years ago, Adam yielded his God-given authority to the devil. The Bible states we become servants of those we obey. Unfortunately, the parents of the human race obeyed Satan and disobeyed God. They ate the forbidden fruit, died spiritually, and lost dominion.

That's why the devil could legitimately offer Jesus, the second Adam, all the kingdoms of the world if He would fall down and worship him. Fortunately, Jesus, unlike Adam, didn't yield to the temptation, or any other one that came along. That's how Jesus could state flatly, "the ruler of this world is coming, and he has nothing in Me." *(John 14:30)*

And today, this destroyer wreaks havoc on the world he rules. Tornadoes, hurricanes and such disasters are not "acts of God". Rather, the Bible tells us God is good and His mercy never ends. *(Psalm 118:1)* It's the evil and merciless devil who inflicts sickness, pain, and every mental and emotional disease on people.

So, don't blame God. Blame Satan for anything that afflicts any part of you, from your person to your pocketbook.

That's the bad news and admittedly a stark scenario.

Now - the good news. Jesus Christ has already overcome the devil. The third letter of the apostle John tells us "The Son of God appeared that He might destroy the works of the devil." *(I John 3:8)*

Jesus Himself encourages us to "take courage; I have overcome the world." *(John 16:33)*

But you may say, "I live in this world, and if the devil is running the system....and my family is getting sick...if I take tranquilizers...get stressed and depressed...what can I do?

First of all, you're beginning to know the truth, and the truth, Jesus said, will set you free. *(John 8:32)* No longer need you be "destroyed for lack of knowledge." *(Hosea 4:6 KJV)*

What's more, as a born-again Christian, you may be in the world, but you can rise above it. Legally, God, through Jesus, has "delivered us from the dominion of darkness and transferred us to the kingdom of His dear Son." *(Colossians 1:13)* Isaiah 53 states that many will be saved through the knowledge of Jesus. And the Greek word for "save" is "sozo", which includes not only being saved from hell, but also protection, deliverance, healing and health.

Notice Jesus' commentary in Luke 13:16 after he healed a woman. "This woman..whom Satan has bound for eighteen long years." Satan bound her, Jesus loosed her.

It's the same today. The devil and his cohorts afflict, Jesus heals through the Holy Spirit as He did then.

The next chapter will show that Jesus already paid in full for your healing and health. Because of what He did, every Christian has a right to be healthy - and every non-Christian should have the opportunity to be healed.

Pay No Charges Ever

" The chastening for our well-being fell upon Him,
And by His scourging we are healed."

(Isaiah 53:5)

It was a pleasant August night in Evansville, Indiana. My wife and I were house guests of good friends we had known since I'd worked in that city.

That evening, all of us visited mutual friends. While we were talking in their living room, I began to get fearful. There was no logical reason for it. But the fear increased. At my request, we left and began driving back.

How I felt sitting in that car is almost inexpressible. Never had I been so gripped with fear. To say it was inordinate would be an understatement. I felt as if I were going under, about to lose my mind.

Back at home base, our host and hostess took action. They spoke to and bound a spirit of fear in the name of Jesus Christ. There was relief. But after my wife and I retired, the attack began again. The evil presence around us was so strong that even my wife's speech became affected. By then, we knew what to do - and began binding the spirit of fear in the name of Jesus Christ. Again, relief came and we were able to sleep. Later , the Lord loosed me from that fearful spirit.

Is fear, indeed, a spiritual force? God's word says in II Timothy 1:7 that we have not been given "the spirit of fear, but of power, and of love, and of a sound mind." *(KJV)*

In a nursing home near us, there was a lady with a severe hearing problem. She used a hearing aid. But when hands were laid on her ears and a spirit of deafness cast out, she could hear well - without her expensive hearing aid. God had just become her hearing aide.

By what right could Faye and I stop a spirit of fear and help unstop a woman's ears. On what grounds can Christians who do such things do them?

Jesus Christ has already paid the price for the health care of everyone in the world. Just prior to His crucifixion,when He was scourged, He took on Himself every sickness, infirmity and pain-physical, mental and emotional. Just as He became our sin substitute and paid the price for our sin, so did He become our sickness substitute. Just as He who was without sin "became sin" for us (*II Corinthians 5:21 KJV*) , He bore on His body and in His mind everything that could harm us physically, mentally and emotionally. Read Isaiah 53:4 & 5, particularly in an amplified version, and refer to scriptures noted in Chapter 3 of this book. Notice in I Peter 2:24, that refers to freeing from both sin and sickness, that "by His wounds you were healed."

Visualize what God in the flesh paid for your health. His back was opened and bleeding from more than forty cat-of-nine-tails-type whip lashes. (pieces of bone were usually included in that kind of vicious scourging.) Yes, the Jews were limited to forty lashes when they scourged, but Jesus was turned over to the Romans, masters of cruelty, who were not restricted by any given limit on the number of lashes. Isaiah 52:14 tells us that Jesus looked like no other man had ever looked. His body must have become like red and "bleeding" hamburger.

In addition, a crown of sharp thorns had been cutting into His head as part of the punishment He bore for your peace of mind. God the Son was emasculated in every way for you and for me.

And this substitutionary suffering , Jesus in place of us, was and is the basic foundation and total payment of the cost of God's Health Care Plan. JESUS PAID IN EVERY WAY SO YOU AND I DON'T HAVE TO PAY IN ANY WAY!

Learn God's Prevention

"I will give you the keys of the kingdom of heaven; and whatever you shall bind on earth shall be bound in heaven." (Matthew 16:19) ("bind", from the Greek, can also be translated "refuse to permit", "shall be bound" can be translated : "shall not be permitted." The phrase "shall be bound" can also be translated "shall have already have been bound.")

God's word tells us His kingdom is right standing with Him and peace and joy in the Holy Spirit. *(Romans 14:17).* Jesus informs us "the kingdom of God is within you." *(Luke 17:21 KJV)* If you're a born-again Christian and you don't have the peace and joy you'd like operating within you, God would like to turn that around.

Early one morning, when I was a rather new Christian, God gave me two words I will never forget.

I was in bed, enjoying a little half-and-half (half-asleep, half-awake). And a stream of negative thoughts began coursing through my mind. Nothing extreme or patently bad, but negative.

Suddenly, before my eyes was a vision that was right to the point. In white letters against a black background were two words that were bold, sharp and clear - DEFEND YOURSELF. God knew that I knew about that first key of the kingdom - the authority to bind or refuse to permit. And I knew He expected me to use it against those demonic, negative thoughts that could affect my day ahead.

After my salvation and filling with the Holy Spirit, the Lord had done a remarkable miracle. He changed me from a negative person (just ask my wife) to a positive one. Through His Spirit and Bible and exceptional teaching, I began to look at the world through God-colored glasses.

The devil, of course, comes only to steal, kill and destroy. *(John 10:10)* Most often, the attack comes in our thought life. That's why God instructs us we should be "taking every thought captive" in line with the mind of Christ. *(II Corinthians 10:5)* Jesus is the master victor and overcomer of all times and He wants His people to be the same way. He didn't go to the cross to raise up a bunch of losers.

Since His resurrection, Jesus has been seated at the right hand of God, the Father, in "heavenly places" (the spirit world) "far above all rule and authority and power and dominion...and He put all things in subjection under His feet and gave Him as head over all things to the church." *(Ephesians 1: 21, 22)* Jesus is now positioned high above the devil and every demon.

So what does that mean to us? He was given as head over all things to US, the church. Now, prepare to get excited, because this concerns every born-again Christian. God, the Father, also "raised us up with Him and seated us with Him in the heavenly places (spirit world) in Christ Jesus." *(Ephesians 2:6)* Good news. The devil is under our feet!

That's not all. Consider the 10th Chapter of the Gospel of Luke. Seventy disciples (not apostles) return to Jesus rejoicing. "Even the demons are subject to us in Your name." *(Luke 10:17)*, they report after He sent them out to teach, preach and heal.

Now, get Jesus' reply. "Behold, I have given you authority to tread upon serpents and scorpions (the devil and his demons) and over all the power of the enemy, and nothing shall injure you." Then He goes on, in Luke 10:20, that, indeed, demons are subject to us. He delegated the use of His awesome authority to fight every invasion of the devil - against body, mind and emotions. Remember what God says in I Thessalonians 5:23. He wants to preserve us spirit , soul and body.

No wonder the Lord wants us to defend ourselves. He's given us what it takes to do it.

Just look at how well God has set up His HMO. We're seated with the victorious Jesus above all demonic forces. They're under our feet and our CEO has ordered us to walk over them, stomp on them, using His authority in His name. As we do, He pours on the power to bind any of them and fend off any attack against any part of ourselves or someone else. The Great Provider (one of God's covenant names is Jehovah Jireh, the Lord Who sees and provides) has made ample provision for our health and welfare. We don't have to pray about it. We already have His word. All we have to do is act on it!

Of course, we can't stop the devil's onslaughts on our own power. We don't have any. But we should be "strong in the Lord and in the power of His might." *(Ephesians 6:10 KJV)* And He's the one who upholds the universe by His powerful word. *(Hebrew 1:3)*

Now look at that mighty name of Jesus we have at our disposal. The name itself means "God Who saves." Philippians 2:9 tells us "Jesus" is the name above every name. And "at the name of Jesus every knee should bow", according to Philippians 2:10. In Mark 16:17, the Lord tells us to use His name against demons. And - in John 17:11, 15, the Lord prayed that God would keep us safe through the power of that name - safe from the evil one.

Now look again at our chapter-heading scripture - that whatever we bind (or refuse to permit) on earth shall have already been bound in heaven. God's done His part, the rest is up to us.

The authority and power to bind or refuse evil will help us "reign in life by one, Christ Jesus." *(Romans 5:17 KJV)* With that key, we can lock out, shut out, the demonic incursions against our mind, body and emotions. Proverbs 18:10 promises "The name of the Lord is a strong tower; the righteous runs into it and is safe." We're to resist harmful thoughts, feelings and physical attacks in the name of Jesus - running to the safety of that strong tower (high above our demonic enemies) and use the key of Matthew 16 (and also *Matthew 18:18*) and "resist the devil" knowing "he will flee" *(James 4:7)*.

How exactly do we do that? We speak to the specific problem and refuse it. Example: "In the name of Jesus, I refuse you, spirit of fear" (or anger, depression, pain, flu or whatever). And, ideally, we keep doing it until the particular problem leaves us.

One afternoon, a lady who had heard this teaching at her nursing home Bible study walked on an elevator of the facility with me. She commented, "It works" She had been rebuking a spirit of fear in the name of Jesus and become less fearful.

One evening, I was teaching at Chicago Teen Challenge. Afterwards, one young man came up and told us he had been coughing during the meeting, but he got the message. And he had quietly refused that spirit in the name of Jesus and the coughing stopped.

This key of binding, or refusing any demonic weapon (including temptation), is so important to God that He happily anticipated it in Psalm 149:8, where we read we are to "bind their kings with chains, and their nobles with fetters of iron; to execute on them the judgment written; this is an honor for all His godly ones." To make this preventive measure even easier for us, Jesus (according to *Colossians*

2:15) has already disarmed the demonic powers. To put the icing on the cake - or the quarantine on the devil - we should know that when we bind or refuse we're moving in agreement with God's word - and in the mouths of two witnesses (His and ours) "every fact will be established." according to II Corinthians 13:1.

Add to all of the above, Jesus' promise that " the Scripture cannot be broken" *(John 10:35)* and you've got an airtight case and the kind of health care prevention program you wont find in any other plan!

The program works very well in emergencies. One Sunday, before going to church, I was hurrying breakfast. To expedite things, I boiled an egg over a high gas flame, putting a metal lid on the pan for speedier heat. When I removed the hot lid, I placed it, bottom up, on the range.

Faye, who began her breakfast a few minutes later, didn't realize the lid was hot - and picked it up. Suddenly, screaming and sobbing, she thrust her hand under cold, running water in the sink. The pain was excruciating, her hand had begun to burn. After getting our composure, we began to refuse spirits of pain, inflammation, swelling and burn, in the name of Jesus.

After about twelve minutes of this, the white area in Faye's hand normalized and the pain was virtually gone. There was no burn.

Using the key of binding or refusing has almost become second nature for us. It can be the same for any Christian who wants to fend off health problems of any sort. God's health care protection is as near as our willingness to use it.

Take God's Cure

"whatever you shall loose on earth shall be loosed in heaven."
(Matthew 16:19)
(The phrase "shall be loosed" can be translated
"shall have already have been loosed.")

Tony lives in one of the nursing homes where our church ministers. One of the most likeable people you'll meet, Tony had become depressed. One Saturday afternoon, I offered to pray for him. And, in Jesus' name, I commanded a spirit of depression to leave him. Tony noticed the difference immediately. He said, "I feel like something left me." And that's exactly what happened.

How many, like Tony, have unknowingly yielded to depression and entered the devil's gloom department?

Deliverance, another name for loosing, is an awesome revelation of the power of God, Who can perform better-than-laser surgery in the twinkling of an eye. Yet, it shouldn't be scary, forbidding or cloaked in some kind of dark mystery. The devil likes to keep us in the dark. Jesus wants us walking in the light. And as Psalm 119:30 informs us, the entrance of God's words bring light. If the word "exorcism" (another term for loosing) makes you think of some kind of priestly ritual, written in a big book, to be used only by special people - think again. Any believer can free himself or someone else from an evil spirit. And Jesus says so in Mark 16:17.

Jesus came to set captives free. In Luke 4:18, he states He was sent to proclaim release to the captives and set free the downtrodden. He's still doing it through His body on earth (God's HMO). It can happen any time any believer believes Jesus' words of Mark 16:17: "These signs shall follow those who believe; in My name they shall cast out demons." This command is in the next-to-the-last sentence of Jesus recorded by Mark. The final sentence in that gospel reports that Jesus confirmed His word with signs that followed. Unless someone wants to hang on to a demon, any true Christian can expel it.

What's the difference between binding or refusing to permit and loosing? Binding renders a demon inoperative, doesn't allow it to function in or against a particular person. Loosing, or casting out, disconnects or forces a spirit to evacuate a particular person. (There also have been many cases of mass deliverance.) Binding usually is effective for a relatively short time. Loosing usually lasts longer - although the spirit may try to return. (More on that later.)

Again, we must emphasize, binding and loosing can be accomplished only in the name of Jesus and only by born-again Christians.

There was a woman, let's call her Kathy, who had been born deaf. As she neared forty, Kathy was still profoundly deaf. One of our most cherished trips to a nursing home was the memorable afternoon when God opened her ears when we cast out that deaf spirit. You should have seen the almost beatific look on her face when she heard sound for the very first time. (How can Saturday afternoon football on TV possibly compare with a sight like that!)

Actually, as one national expert on the subject has written, deaf spirits are among the easiest to eject and the quickest to try to return. In the case of Kathy, a young lady with no knowledge of her authority in the name of Jesus, the spirit sneaked back. Then through an interpreting friend of hers, we told her she could speak the words of hearing for herself. She got the message, but not all of it. As I recall, she said, "Spirit of deafness get out." Nothing happened. She had forgotten to use the name of Jesus. Then when she commanded the spirit leave "in the name of Jesus", she began to beam. She could hear again.

There's tremendous power in that name. Another lady had a sore foot. When the spirit was told to go in the name of Jesus, the pain left her. She told us, "When you said "Jesus" it was like a zap hit my foot." The Holy Spirit doesn't fool around .

In another nursing home lived a very sweet lady in her seventies. One of her eyes was totally blind and had been for four years. Laying a hand on that eye, we commanded a blind spirit to leave in the name of Jesus. When the hand was removed from her eye, we almost automatically asked if she felt (or noticed) anything. She answered with three little words Faye and I will never forget —"I can see." Several years later she was still seeing through both eyes.

Earlier this year, I was on the phone, complaining about a service problem that shouldn't have occurred. I began to get upset and a little nasty. Then when I talked to God about it (internally), He showed me it was a spirit of irritability. As soon as I told it to leave in Jesus' name, my attitude changed. I was more relaxed and peaceful. After I apologized to the party on the line and confessed the sin to God, I again realized the Lord wants us loosed from anything that would try to control us.

During one vacation, Faye and I visited her dad in Central Ohio. One of her relatives was also visiting. This eminently likeable Christian in her eighties (who didn't look it) mentioned a long-standing back problem that caused discomfort and the need to wear special shoes. Learning she had spinal curvature, we cast out a spirit of scoliosis. She quickly noticed the difference. Weeks later she wrote to tell us the back problem no longer existed. Whatever we loose on earth will be loosed by heaven.

Perhaps you may think it almost presumptuous to speak with the authority of Jesus Christ. But, consider this. Isn't believing the word of God (the Bible) and acting on it really humility? To say God is wrong, that we can't or shouldn't do what He tells us to do is really a form of pride. We're exalting our opinion over His word.

If we let "religious" thinking stop us and reject the articles of God's health insurance, we (and those we could help) will certainly not share in its benefits. Christians haven't rejected God's promise of salvation and eternal life through faith in His word - or they wouldn't have become Christians. Why then should Christians reject God's provision for walking in Jesus' hard-won victory over the devil - which is also enunciated in the same Bible?

Deliverance from and rejection of whatever demonic force that's hurting people is healthy - and the facilitating factor in the world's most effective health care plan.

Often, binding and loosing can be used in the same situation. An elderly lady at a local nursing home found it very painful to raise one of her arms more than about two feet. She didn't like to do it and you couldn't blame her. Two of us from Good News Church offered to pray for her. And we did command suspected spirits, including arthritis , to leave her. No relief. We then realized from her comments the lady didn't believe anything was going to happen.

The next time we had a Bible study in that nursing home, we again offered help to that same lady. Only this time, one of us addressed the appropriate spirit of infirmity while the other was binding spirits of doubt. It worked. The lady was able to raise her arm higher with no pain.

I had an opportunity to pray for someone who had terminal cancer. Laying my hand on him, I told the cancer spirit to go, cursed the cancer and commanded every cancer cell to die. It was to no effect, then or later. This man, unfortunately, was loaded with doubt. His mind was preoccupied with the medical treatment and possibilities, not the spiritual potential. In this case, binding a spirit of doubt was essential. I didn't do it. God's hands were tied. In a matter of months the man passed away.

Many people bind just prior to casting out. This can keep a spirit from manifesting before it has to leave. Jesus said *(Matthew 12:29)* that one cant enter the strong man's house unless he first ties him up. Just prior to this, He speaks of driving out demons by the spirit of God. Most of the time, Faye and I bind first, although at times we forget and God still takes over. We must remember that the Third Person of the Trinity is the Holy Spirit, not the legalistic spirit.

The VanVoorhis family lives the scriptures daily. They believe the word of God all the way - and constantly bind and loose. As a result, dad, mom and the four children have been amazingly healthy. In fact, only once in the past twelve years did any of them have to see a doctor or get medication.

Late one afternoon, Mark, around ten years old, became totally blind. The infirmity had begun some days earlier and had reached the "total" stage - no sight from either eye. Both eyes were bloodshot, his lids were swollen and there was pain.

At this flood stage, Mark's dad took his authority - as a believer and as the head of his family . He commanded a spirit of infirmity to leave his son in the name of Jesus.

The next morning, Mark was lying on the sofa listening to Christian music. And he heard a voice speak to him. It said , "Stand up. You're healed." As he obeyed, he was instantly healed. The swelling, pain and redness left. And his sight was totally restored.

In this faith-filled family, parents and kids, now ranging to adulthood, rebuke colds, sore throats and anything that may come along. God honors their faith and comes through again and again. Their active participation in God's small-group plan has saved them thousands of dollars in medical and doctor bills.

Binding and loosing - prevention and cure of whatever ails you or anybody else. Jesus has given every born-again Christian these keys to health maintenance. There is only one requirement - use them!

Know What Induces It

"be in good health, just as your soul prospers."
(III John 2)

In her family and among her friends, Joanne is known to be a powerful prayer warrior. When she prays, she does it with great faith and confidence. When she confronts demons, she expects results.

Joanne enhanced her standing when she dealt with a long-standing problem that had been bugging her niece, Maxine.

The young lady was a college student who was loaded with pressure, and like so many Americans today, she had become stressed out. She had reached a point where she was vomiting again and again. She couldn't eat.

Maxine had gone to the doctor on campus. The problem persisted. Finally, she came home. In desperation, she went to her family doctor.

When she returned home from the doctor's office, her aunt Joanne and her mother were in the kitchen. As she looked at her pale, sick and frustrated niece, Joanne asked, "Do you want to get rid of that?" The girl was more than willing.

That's when Joanne took authority in the name of Jesus Christ. She commanded a spirit of stress to leave the girl. What happened, she, the girl and the mother will never forget.

All three ladies heard an audible and loud "Whoosh" as the spirit left. Maxine's eyes were wide as saucers. She felt different. She was relaxed. No more did the vomiting and inability to eat continue. She was able to go back to college and go on with life - because her aunt knew Jesus meant what He said when in Mark 16:17 He commanded her to cast out demons in His name.

A few years ago, a major publication reported that 25% of the U.S. work force had anxiety. No doubt this vast group didn't know or believe what Jesus said about not being anxious about a thing because the same God who clothed the lilies of the field is well able to care for His children.

Anxiety, like his first cousin, fear, is a spirit and can be dealt with accordingly. Almost all of us, I suspect, have had it come at us. Sometimes, my wife will wake up with a pain in the back of her head. But she's discovered that when she vigorously rebukes a spirit of anxiety the pain goes.

Kristi, a young actress we know wanted help with recurring migraine headaches. She was entertaining one at the time. However, when Faye and I commanded a spirit of migraine headache to depart, it didn't do it. Then, after asking a few questions, we felt that a spirit of stress and one of anger or even resentment was involved. After we spoke to them, Kristi relaxed. Then we took authority over the spirit of migraine headache and this time it took off taking its pain with it.

One night, after the service in her church, Iris wanted prayer for pain around her liver. However the pain wouldn't leave her until the emotional blockers were removed.

Iris, like so many in today's selfish society had been put down and rejected. And for years, she had to put up with the spirits that gained access as a result. Armed with this knowledge, fellow Christians commanded spirits of rejection and fear of rejection to leave. After that happened (and she felt noticeably better), it was possible to command an inherited spirit of liver infirmity (it ran in her family) to get out. It did and so did the pain in Iris' body.

A specialist in holding spiritual seminars in a Southern state told me that rejection has been the most common problem these seminars have come across. Our experience has proved that , time after time, rejection and the fear of it happening again have been spirits blocking physical healing - or simply keeping people from being more successful in life.

Marty heads the children's ministry at his church. Normally a picture of health, he was having trouble hearing on one Sunday morning. He had become deaf in his left ear. The deafness had gone on for many hours.

Staff members in the church tried casting out a deaf spirit. To no avail. Then they prayed for guidance and the Holy Spirit indicated a spirit of anger was involved. Also, Marty had been under unusual pressure in recent days; stress had invaded him. With this knowledge, the staff members cast out spirits of anger and stress. Marty could tell something had happened; he felt more calm. But the clogging and lack of hearing continued. What other spirits were involved? Prompted by the Holy Spirit, the prayers tried something they had never heard of before. They cast out any spirits of clogging and blockage - and Marty's hearing cleared up!

God had healed Marty's physical problem. But, first, those emotional spirits had to be ejected. The ear problem had been "emotionally induced."

Stephanie was totally deaf in her left ear. Her half-hearing had continued for years. She was missing parts of conversations. Often, she'd have to lean her head in the right direction to understand better.

Normally, deaf spirits are among the easiest to cast out. But, with hands-on prayer and a command to leave in the name of Jesus Christ, the hearing loss remained. Discussion revealed Stephanie was quick to blame and condemn herself. Sometimes it seemed she couldn't do a thing right - or so she thought. That's when her Christian cohorts decided to cast out a spirit of self-condemnation - and Stephanie felt lighter and better.

With self-condemnation gone, hands were laid on Stephanie again and the deaf spirit was commanded to leave. Then the hearing came back to her left ear. First, the emotionally-blocking spirit had to be removed - then God's healing took place.

So often, we and many others more experienced than we are, have seen spirits of anger, fear, anxiety, stress, tension, rejection and others block mental and/or physical healing. It seems that such spirits would open the door to other invaders and guard that open door until they were removed.

Sometimes, it's easy to see the cause, but it's not so easy to tell someone you don't know, "Look, you have a problem with anger that has to be eliminated before God can go further." Yet, caregivers in God's Health Care Plan have to consider the hurting enough to have the guts to offer what may be a hard-to-swallow prescription.

There's a major insurance company that for years has been known for its use of an umbrella as a symbol of protection for policyholders covered by that company. Of course, if a policy holder let his insurance lapse long enough, that umbrella of coverage was removed.

Every born-again Christian automatically gets under God's protective umbrella from the second of that new birth. But, in order to receive all of the benefits, including protection, his covenant with God provides, he must know how to operate in the word of God (the Bible). Binding and loosing, as we've pointed out earlier, are keys the Lord has given us to access his health care for ourselves and others. If we don't use them, the devil can rain on our parade.

Also, disobedience to God's word can get us out from under his umbrella. Sin separates us from God,, until we confess it. In Exodus 15:26, God identifies Himself as our Healer. But if we don't shape up and keep our part of the contract, He doesn't have to keep His.

Can the devil and company lay sickness and pain on us even if we're not in unconfessed sin? Sure, if we let him and don't refuse the temptation to get sick just as we refuse the temptation to sin. If someone gets sick or doesn't get healed, it doesn't mean he's in sin. He, or someone else, isn't using the name of Jesus so God can move in and handle the problem.

But, let's take another look at what God calls sin. It's more than breaking the Commandments or not doing something you know to do. Anything that is contrary to God's word (scriptures), is sin.

God says in the Bible, over and over, not to be afraid, for He is with us. Therefore, if we accept the temptation to fear, we have sinned.

God hates doubt. Eve was conned by Satan into disbelieving God and she (and we) suffered the consequences. Jesus said more than once, "Why did you doubt?" Since Christians are to live by faith (*Hebrews 10:38*), then disbelieving or doubting God's word is sin. A highly-respected Bible teacher seems right on in calling fear and doubt the most common sins of Christians.

When I was a baby Christian (at the tender age of 55), my wife, our youngest son and I were on retreat at a CFO (Camp Farthest Out) in Fulton, Missouri. It was in a speech in Fulton that Winston Churchill first used the phrase "the iron curtain," which of course referred to the solid veil dropped around its empire by the then Soviet Union.

One night, while at the retreat, the Lord gave me a short dream that would help lift my own curtain of ignorance. In the dream, two masked men were approaching us, one from one side, the second from the other side. Then, in that dream, I told the masked men to get out in the name of Jesus. The men changed direction and walked by us instead of into us. What did it mean? As I prayed asking God for an interpretation, I understood the masked men were the twin bandits of faith - fear and doubt. And how often do they come in sheep's clothing!

Consider a couple of other sins that you may not have considered as such.

They're the one-two-step to the emotional basement: discouragement and depression. In the Book of Joshua, 1:8, God commands Joshua (and us) not to be discouraged or afraid, for He is with us. In Isaiah 61:3 KJV, God gives us the garment of praise for the spirit of heaviness (which also can be translated "depression").

Too often we forget to start praising God instead of sinking into a demonically-induced emotional quagmire that could open the floodgate to a spirit of suicide.

If we allow the enemy's negative thoughts to enter us, that evil spirit who's been knocking on the outside can come in.

Refuse to take the thought in the first place, "Watch over your heart with all diligence, for from it flow the springs of life." (*Proverbs 4:23*)

Too often, though, a person is not aware of being attacked by or captive to fear, doubt, depression, discouragement, or other common spirits such as anger, resentment, self-pity, rejection, etc. Often, also, spirits may be inherited. Dad may have had a hot temper. Your aunt, like one of mine, may have always been startled when she heard the doorbell. To help yourself or someone from getting bogged down by blocking spirits, pray to God for revelation, or ask others in the body of Christ (fellow-Christians) who may see something you don't.

God doesn't want us to suffer from "emotionally-induced" sickness, or slavery to demonically-induced emotions, either!

And, He's the only health care provider to provide a way out.

See What God Has Wrought

"And men shall speak of the power of Thine awesome acts"
(Psalm 145:6)

The cause of all physical disease and mental malease wants us to be ignorant of his devices and how to defuse them.

One evening in the early 1980s, our family was having supper prior to a gathering of students at a videotape version of Charles and Frances Hunter's School of Ministry that met weekly in our home.

As the meal went on, I became increasingly uncomfortable. Fluish symptoms surfaced and I was close to a chill. Quickly finishing supper, I went to the bedroom, closed the door and began to fight, using the weapons of righteousness, the name of Jesus and the word of God.

Feeling even worse, I was angry at the devil. I began pacing the floor, commanding any spirits of influenza, chill, infirmity and anything else that seemed to fit to leave me. Over and over, I spoke the name of Jesus and threw in a variety of healing and authority scriptures - all aimed at an enemy who was out to make me sick and miss the upcoming meeting in our living room.

After at least twenty minutes of constantly rebuking and scripture-quoting, I began to feel better and in minutes was back to normal. God had delivered me from the attack just in time to make the meeting.

Shortly before popping the first video into the VCR, I looked at the titles on the tape. One of them concerned casting out demons, a second covered a somewhat similar area. The afflicter didn't want me at the meeting and didn't like what would be revealed there. (He still doesn't want Christians to know he and his minions are subject to them.) But, fortunately, he didn't prevail. Instead, all of us went on to learn much about the casting out of demons, based on scripture and the Hunters' wide knowledge and experience.

Since that time, Faye and I have become more knowledgeable and proficient in resisting and uprooting the enemy in our lives and the lives of others. And in the years that have followed, we've experienced and come across a wide variety of examples of the freeing and

31

healing power of God vested in the name of Jesus Christ. Hopefully, what we share in the rest of this chapter (and book) will enlighten and encourage you. These examples should make it eminently clear that God's Health Care Plan is no paper tiger, and that it works time after time, place after place - in all kinds of health problems.

UNTIMELY SLEEP AND CHRONIC FATIGUE

One evening, after a three-hour session of the above-mentioned video school, one of the ladies, (a former airline stewardess), told us she always seemed to get sleepy while she was reading and that 90% of her reading was the Bible. This would happen even in the middle of the day. As we sought the Lord, praying in tongues, the words "spirit of stupor" came to my mind. Faye then commanded a spirit of stupor to leave the lady. We were amazed at what happened. The ex-stewardess, who had been comfortably settled back in her chair, bolted upright almost instantly. She felt more alert and clear-minded. Later she reported that she no longer was getting sleepy when she read the Bible. No longer could that spirit keep her from it.

Fred was having problems in his business. He was getting sleepy at the strangest times, finding it difficult to concentrate. The cause was narcolepsy. The way out was God's health care provision. A fellow-Christian called him one evening and learned of the situation. And he decided to do something about it. With Fred's permission, a spirit of narcolepsy was commanded to leave him, in the name of Jesus Christ. Later, Fred reported the narcolepsy was gone. He could work unimpeded.

Bob works out of his home. He's middle-aged, runs and is very healthy. But about three years ago, his life (and work) was affected by the need to nap, not occasionally, but daily at about 5 P.M., at least Monday through Friday. Bob didn't like it, but he didn't know what to do about it. He was getting enough sleep.

That was the problem. Here's the solution. We had heard about that much-publicized phenomenon, Chronic Fatigue Syndrome. (Even a major news magazine featured the disease on as its cover story.) At our home Bible fellowship, we felt that, as in every other disease, there was a demon involved. So, in the meeting when Bob divulged his nap syndrome, we commanded any spirit of Chronic Fatigue Syndrome to leave Bob, in Jesus' name.

Two weeks later, Bob reported he no longer needed to take his daily nap, or even a weekly one. The chronic fatigue was gone. Three years later, although he is under greater pressure, there has been no recurrence. And Bob doesn't expect to be caught napping that way again

God's word promises us sweet sleep *(Proverbs 3:24)*. But not when we don't want it!

ALCOHOL, NICOTINE AND DRUGS

Probably no other substance has had such an adverse effect on society as alcohol. Shattered lives, broken families, highway accidents and deaths. Alcohol collects a high toll. It's an empty, temporary and dangerous escape from reality. Certainly, it's one of Satan's most destructive weapons. Even here, God's power is infinitely greater.

Notice, for example, how He worked through Larry and friends. Larry Naselli and two Christian comrades were revisiting the residence of two new converts. There they also found a visitor who was flagrantly drunk and incoherent and interruptive. But he did allow the visiting trio to pray for him. They laid hands on him, and, in the name of Jesus, they took authority over the situation. The alcohol and its effects were commanded to leave the man.

Immediately, the man broke into a heavy sweat. Someone brought him a towel. Even before he could fully dry off - in about twenty seconds - he was stone sober. He was also appreciative of what God had done for him and rededicated his life to Jesus Christ.

Elizabeth had been a chain smoker for years. Her clothing reeked of tobacco. Her desire was to get free. So one Sunday morning in the back of our church, she agreed to prayer. The assistant pastor at that time commanded the demon of nicotine to leave. It did, and Elizabeth began to cry. What she couldn't do, God had accomplished. Years later, with the desire to smoke gone, Elizabeth continued to be smoke free.

Virginia is a hard-working and conscientious lady whose family was having short-term financial problems. Overly-concerned, she had gotten into fear, anxiety and depression over what looked to her like an almost impossible situation.

Her turnaround began after she was freed from several spirits in the name of Jesus Christ. One of them was a spirit you might not think existed. Among the medications she had been taking was cortisone, a common steroid that can mask painful symptoms. In what apparently was a word of knowledge from the Lord, the idea came to one of the prayers involved to address a spirit of cortisone.

What happened was eye-opening. After the spirit was spoken to, Virginia felt something she had not felt for some time. She suddenly became quite tired! The cortisone apparently had prevented this, allowing, along with other causes, Virginia to reach the edge of what used to be called a nervous breakdown.

Fortunately, the crisis ended and Virginia got better. Equally fortunate, was her knowledge of God's word and her God given authority. As she went on to fight the demonic incursion, and as steps were taken to ease the problem, both she and the situation improved.

Shortly after I gave my life to Jesus Christ, I was still taking small doses of valium. One day, at a charismatic meeting, I stopped at the drinking fountain to take that daily dose of the popular tranquilizer. As I was raising it to my lips, a quiet voice within me seemed to say, "You don't need that." I lowered the valium from my lips. That was the end of any drug dependence. After more than sixteen years, I still don't need it.

God doesn't care for habit-forming drugs, alcohol or nicotine. His health care provision would dispense with all of them.

FEAR, ANXIETY, TENSION AND STRESS

Fear has torment, God warns in I John 4:18. Psalm 34:4 promises that when we seek God, he'll deliver us out of it. He did it for me (as I recount in another chapter) and he did for the following people.

A friend of ours brought his niece to church one night for help. Verna, still in her twenties, was unable to work. She was gripped with fear. Wisely, she was seeking help and saw a psychiatrist regularly.

As her uncle and I prayed in the spirit, I saw the word DELIVER-ANCE flash across my consciousness. God was making it clear this was the time to do something. (Neither of us, back then, were as familiar with that provision of God's health care as we are today.) So we proceeded to cast the spirit of fear from the girl. And the dark ness left her face. She was brighter.

Two weeks later, Verna was visited by her uncle. She was happy and smiling as she told him, "Uncle, I'm not afraid anymore." Freed from fear, she was able to get back to work.

Denise, normally a very positive and upbeat member of our church, was sad - and she called for prayer. Someone close to her was in the hospital and near death. And even though she knew he was a Christian and headed for heaven, she had become fearful about the impending death. That didn't have to be, so a spirit of fear was commanded to leave her and it left. How did Denise know she was free? She immediately noticed a difference in the way she felt. And as she glanced at the mirror near her, she observed that her expression had changed. She was smiling!

One night, Mona weathered a frightful demonic test. Her husband was out of town on business and she was alone in the house. She lay in bed , reading her Bible until she fell asleep.

Waking up later, she felt a strange presence in the room. Beyond that, she felt a hand "grabbing my ankles." She began to shake. Otherwise she felt paralyzed, unable to move. Then she remembered what she had heard about her spiritual authority. She should tell any demonic intruder to get out in the name of Jesus. But, Mona couldn't open her mouth to do it. That's when she spoke the command in her mind. And she heard an audible voice so loud and commanding it seemed to shake the house. This Voice spoke the same words Mona had spoken mentally - but with undeniable authority - "In the name of Jesus, leave!" Mona's face relaxed, the unseen but felt demonic grip began to leave. After Mona herself gave the same command audibly, the shaking and paralysis stopped. She was freed from it. The ordeal had ended. God had worked wonders in the emergency room.

Imagine being so fearful you wouldn't go out the front door of your house without clinging to your spouse. For years, Rebecca was bound by that kind of fear. But, providentially, God's Health Care Plan covers emotional health. And one day she discovered that as her pastor took authority over her emotional enemies, casting them out in the name of Jesus.

Happy ending: today, Rebecca isn't afraid to go out alone. In fact, she's so outgoing, she's become the second largest producer of a major real estate company.

I had been believing God would prosper us and was speaking His word on the subject. Then, one Sunday evening during praise and worship at church, the idea came to mind to pray for a particular client of mine. I did that.

Roughly two weeks later, I called that client. We talked about examples of my audio/visual writing. Shortly afterward, this client offered me a chance to write a major project that he had been given. Never before, since I had been writing , had such a lucrative project come my way. However, this was a very demanding client and not easy to work for. And I asked for an hourly rate beyond what he was willing to pay - and lost the project, which would have brought in enough to pay off all of our credit card and other debt.

Fear that the project would be too massive for me to handle was a major factor in my decision. God knew I could do it - he sent it in.

Days later, I could have reversed that decision. As I sat by my phone, I realized fear was involved and I commanded a spirit of fear to leave me. Suddenly and involuntarily, one hand moved to the phone, in a ready position to make the call. But, I let the fear come back and join other deterring spirits.

I never did make that call to start reaping the reward God had provided. Fear says you can't. God says you can.

Fear. Anxiety. Worry. That unholy trio began to harass Cynthia, the wife of a pastor of a Midwestern church. She had become overly concerned about affairs of the church. And, as she tells it, one day, as she was sitting on her sofa, she started to feel "strange" and "spooky". For no apparent reason, tremendous anxiety came upon her bringing almost unbearable torment.

As best she could, Cynthia began rebuking the attacking spirits in the name of Jesus. But, there was no immediate relief. In the early morning, she finally fell asleep. Yet, when she awoke, the mental oppression was still with her.

Fear gripped Cynthia. She was afraid to drive, afraid to go out. And the normally friendly lady had become paranoid. Because she was also a nurse, Cynthia was fearful of going to the emergency room of a hospital. They might lock her up. She knew she was on the edge of a nervous breakdown.

When she resisted the devil's attacks, why didn't he flee from her according to James 4:7? Cynthia realized her level of faith had dropped. In recent days, she hadn't prayed or read her Bible. She had become too busy. So she began to immerse herself in scriptures. She prayed much in tongues and built herself up spiritually. And, as her faith rose, her resistance against the tormenting spirits was more authoritative. The mental attack, which had already begun to diminish, began a fast fade.

After twelve days of suffering, Cynthia was free. The torment was gone. And the usually cool and confident pastor's wife had regained her composure and her mental health. More than a year later, Cynthia is doing fine and recently has delivered her third child. (She was not pregnant at the time of the mental attack.)

Cynthia could have knuckled under to the devil's barrage. Today she could be in a mental hospital or ward. Instead, she's still in the mainstream helping her husband, her family and other people.

Days in God's intensive care prevented years of costly mental care.

Lana was having arguments with her husband and she wanted help. We spoke to a contentious spirit and several others. But there was no apparent major change. But when we commanded a spirit of control to leave, the battle began. The spirit manifested increasingly as Lana sat erect with her hands clenched as if she were at the controls, tightly in charge. Her face showed tense resolve, so did her body, as her hands and arms seemed to grip those invisible controls.

Then we discovered another spirit was involved. Fear. (How often does it seem to be the bottom-line bugaboo!) Next, ensued an even lengthier battle before Lana was freed. The fear showed itself. It clung to Lana because she was afraid to be without it. Finally, she let go and so did the spirit of fear.

Fear can lead to trying to take control as a protective measure. Lana's arguments with her husband were because she felt she had to be in control - and have the last word. And that kind of spirit can bring resentment and conflict where other people are concerned. It's bad news.

Lana's good marriage began to get even better and with fear handled, she's become more able to speak even before groups.

And she's on her way to a more satisfying and productive life.

Anxiety is sneaky. It can latch on to you while you're busy and concentrating. While I was writing this book, I realized I had become uptight. That's when I told a spirit of anxiety and one of inherited anxiety (my mother often had been anxious) to leave me. They did, and I relaxed into a semi-slumped position and spoke the scripture, "The Lord shall be my confidence." *(Proverbs 3:26)*

When I did that, almost involuntarily, I unbuttoned the sweater I was wearing in my warm office. Perhaps I had also become anxious about getting cold. In any event, anxiety can be restricting and emotionally unpleasant. With God's health care coverage, we don't have to put up with it.

Recently, we spoke on the phone to an old friend. It was a pleasure to reminisce, but knowing her husband was fighting a dread disease brought an unspoken heaviness to the conversation. The lady herself was bothered with a kidney infection. We commanded any such spirit to leave, but nothing happened. Then, realizing she was under severe pressure because of her husband's illness, we spoke to spirits of anxiety, fear, stress and tension. There was a marked change. She became relaxed, her voice sounded better.

After those blockers were removed, we commanded that spirit of infirmity to leave her body - and our friend felt the power of God in her body. The healing had begun.

Matt's elderly dad was in a nursing home. Faithfully, many days a week, Matt visited his dad whose health and awareness was gradually worsening. And when you're already 100 years old, there isn't a long way to go.

So Matt called a relative in another state for prayer. Faced with the daily pressure and what seemed like a no-win situation, he had become depressed and quite tense.

The Christian relative recalls commanding spirits of depression and stress to leave in Jesus' name. After tension was also cast out, Matt felt much better. He experienced tremendous relief.

Then, armed with the knowledge he could resist those same spirits if they attacked him again, he was in a stronger position to cope with his dad's situation without being sapped by an onslaught from the health-destroyer.

Bonnie is not a complainer. Fortunately, just before she left our home Bible fellowship one night, she admitted she had shooting pains that were raging from her neck to her shoulders. This had been going on for some time.

Now, Bonnie was an automobile broker. She bought cars at auctions and resold them to dealers. That's a demanding occupation in pretty much of a man's world. In fact, Bonnie may have been the only female in the city to buy at used car auctions and resell. So, it was evident she was undergoing stress.

Of course, stress is a normal part of everyday life, isn't it? The answer to that seemingly rhetorical question is - it doesn't have to be. Stress is just as demonic as any bondage from any other evil spirit that would keep us from the more abundant life Jesus came to give us.

We felt the Lord wanted us to do something about Bonnie's painful state by helping Him deliver her out of it. And, in the name of Jesus, we commanded a spirit of stress to leave her. Away it went, and the young lady reported that 75% of the pain was gone. Her roommate remarked that her face looked a lot better.

A listener to a by-phone radio station interview called from an eastern state. She thought I was in her city and we might have a prayer meeting where she could get help from God. Since she was about a thousand miles away, that was unfeasible. But I was able to pray on the phone. She was having emotional difficulties. Anxiety and depression seemed to get on her easily and often .

Since God's health care delivery system knows no mileage barriers, both spirits were easily ejected in Jesus name in less than two minutes. After anxiety left, the listener felt better. When the spirit of depression took off, she reported feeling lighter. Isaiah 61:3 (KJV) calls depression "a spirit of heaviness." It was a simple loosing. No incantations or mumbo jumbo. Not even any anguished prayer. Jesus did it through the Holy Spirit; confirming His word with signs following.

Betty's son went into the emergency room of a hospital in great pain. The culprit was appendicitis. On the operating table, it was discovered the appendix had already ruptured. The operation was successful. Yet the concerned mother had become anxious. She also began to feel symptoms of indigestion.

The physicians who removed the son's appendix could not, of course, remove the mother's anxiety and indigestion. That's where God's health care kicked in. Learning the situation during a phone from Betty, a Christian friend cast out a spirit of anxiety. Betty felt lighter.

Then a spirit of fear left. More relief. After a spirit of worry departed, she was more relaxed. With the emotional spirits out of the way, the spirit of indigestion was rebuked. And the pressure left Betty's body. God had rejuvenated one of his daughters.

APPENDICITIS

Is appendicitis itself demonic? A Chicago-area dentist we'll call Ray can tell you.

Ray received training in oral surgery in a county hospital in a southern state where he was rotated through other medical services at the facility. And because he was well aware of the symptoms of appendicitis, he knew what was attacking his body when those symptoms came on him.

On that memorable Saturday, and especially that night, Ray suffered increasingly excruciating pain. He was racked with fever. But Ray, a born-again Christian, was very conversant with God's healing promises in scriptures. He had prayed for patients in his office and God had healed many.

And so, the middle-aged dentist decided to stand his ground and fight - rather than be hospitalized with what he terms "undiagnosed appendicitis."

As Ray tells it, the battle began at about 7 P.M. that Saturday night. He took authority over the devil in the name of Jesus. He bound and loosed Satan, spirits of pain, appendicitis and anything else that seemed appropriate. And he kept speaking healing scriptures. "I became very angry", Ray says. He was angry at the pain, the appendicitis and the devil. He shouted at his spiritual enemies, rebuking them and filling his bedroom with God's word on the subject. Finally at 4 A.M., Ray fell asleep.

A little later, he dragged himself out of bed, determined to get to church for the Sunday morning service. But, feeling terrible, Ray arrived late, near the end of the service. As he walked up the church steps, Ray was talking to God. He was asking, "How will the pastor know I have undiagnosed appendicitis that is healed?"

When, battle-weary and hurting, Ray dropped into the pew, the pastor had already finished preaching. A few minutes later, looking out over the congregation, Ray's pastor announced, "Someone here has undiagnosed appendicitis that is healed."

Astounded at this word of knowledge from the pastor who knew nothing of his problem, Ray, still feeling terrible, but happy that God had confirmed his claim of healing, got into his car and drove home.

Gradually, the pain subsided, and Ray never did have to go into the hospital and have his formerly-flaming appendix removed. God had healed him, honoring the stand he took in the name of Jesus and his refusal to quit, believing God's promise and using Jesus' name again and again against his demonic enemies, until they left and God healed.

Ray had fought what the Bible calls "the good fight of faith" (*I Timothy 6:12 KJV*) and won. Jehovah Jireh, His Provider, had seen and provided the health care he needed.

Shortly afterward, Ray was treated for pinworms, and it was noted that pinworms could be a cause of appendicitis.

CONFUSION

The elimination of health hazards is not exactly an exact science as far as the caregiver is concerned.

At a nursing home for the mentally ill, we wanted to help a resident who was shaking on one side of his body. As I recall, we took authority over spirits of fear and anxiety and there was little apparent relief. From ministering to the man on other occasions, we knew he was prone to confusion. So we went on to command a spirit of confusion to leave him.

To our surprise, the shaking stopped. At once. Obviously, there was a connection between the shaking and confusion. What it was, we don't know. We do know that the man, made aware of the demonic cause of that problem, can refuse that spirit himself, in case of future incursions.

GRIEF

We like to make room visits in nursing homes and pray for people. On one such expedition, I stopped to see a lady who was in bed with some kind of ailment. As we talked, she mentioned that her husband of many years had died about two weeks earlier. She had been grieving almost constantly and wished she could stop it. After all, she knew her husband, also a Christian, was in heaven with Jesus - and even happier than he had been with her.

What to do? Get to the heart of the problem. I had never done it before, but what was there to lose? So, in the name of Jesus Christ, a spirit of grief was commanded to leave this child of God. Quickly, the lady brightened. And she reported that the fluttering in her stomach had ceased. As I left the room, she was joyful, almost tearfully, praising and thanking God, with her hands raised in the air.

Her inner healing was scriptural. According to Isaiah 53, Jesus Christ has already borne our griefs, so we don't have to.

ANGER

In the early years of nursing home ministry, Faye and I learned by experience about the antidote for anger. Just before we were to begin a Bible study at a local facility, a fight broke out between two of the residents. One lady was trying to claw another lady. Not only would this physical battle prove a hindrance to the meeting, but someone was likely to get hurt.

Fortunately, we had enough presence of mind to bind that spirit of anger. This paralyzed the spirit and the fighting stopped. All was calm.

Anger, we've discovered, is a very prevalent spirit in nursing homes, especially in the mental homes, where residents are commonly suffering from some form of schizophrenia or are manic-depressive.

Of course, it's no secret that anger is a prevalent problem outside of nursing homes as well. Many of us have to contend with it. Zach found that anger was having an adverse effect on his marriage. And he wanted that marriage to improve. So, a humble man, he was quick to let us take action - even in the midst of a group of fellow Christians.

When that spirit of anger was cast out, Zach felt a warmth in his body. Undoubtedly it was the Holy Spirit gently manifesting. Zach had been delivered, and even though he had to stand against the return of that spirit, he's been able to be more patient and less volatile and an even better husband to his wife.

Sometimes, the Holy Spirit moves on someone very visibly. This happened during the Good News Church prison ministry. One of the young men we'll call Mac was unhappy about how his outbursts of anger were affecting his relationship with a good friend - not to mention other people. For no known reason, he would suddenly break out in great anger.

When I spoke to that spirit of anger, I felt I should lay one hand on Mac's forehead. The power of God hit him and he reeled backwards, dropping on to the floor. (God will do whatever is necessary to perform a successful operation.)

After Mac got up, he knew he had undergone a change. And he seemed appreciative and joyful. God loves prisoners - and they need our love, too!

When someone is bound by a spirit, that person may be blinded and unaware of it. Martha came to a home meeting one night and needed deliverance from a spirit of anger. But, when the problem was mentioned to her, she became angry and insisted she had no such problem. The anger was, of course, showing itself and didn't want to leave. Instead, when Martha left, that spirit went with her. God gives us free choice. Martha had made hers.

REBELLION AND OTHER CHILD MOLESTERS

Some deliverances take a while. Yet even though this freeing of a bound individual covered more than a half hour, God loosed him from spirits that had affected him for years.

In this case, the hurting teenage boy was at home, miles away, but the parents were in our living room. They related a group of problems that harassed the young man. He couldn't seem to shake them off. These included anger and many others that were retarding his progress.

Faye and I and the parents prayed and spirits of anger, fear, swearing, envy and rebellion were commanded to leave the boy in the name of Jesus. And the Lord, as He often does, added to the diagnosis. He gave the mother a vision of a tiny, whimpering spirit - self-pity. This malefactor was then kicked out in the name of the Lord.

Later, one of the parents told us their teenage son was much better. God considers parents authorities over their children and wants them to protect them.

And He's waiting to help them do it.

One parent who knows how to improve his home environment is Garth, a pastor who practices what he preaches. Not only does he tell others about the authority they have in Jesus Christ, but he exercises that authority with his own children.

Sometimes Garth's kids would get rebellious, talk back, refuse to do things, get their hackles up. (Sound familiar?) That's when Garth would deal with spirits of rebellion. He'd bind the spirit affecting his progeny, commanding it to get off and, if necessary, to get out of that child.

Did it work? Garth reports there was a noticeable change. The next time he talked with his young people, "they were sweet".

As a well-known comedian of earlier decades would have rejoined, "How sweet it is!" Families invariably run more smoothly when parents subscribe to God's Health Care Plan.

Our granddaughter is normally a happy, pleasant , easy-to-get-along-with child. But, like any two-and-a-half-year-old, she can have her moments.

On this particular morning, the young lady threw a tantrum. She was angry, demanding and very vocal. Rather than give in, spank her or just suffer, I decided to use my authority. And in the name of Jesus, I bound spirits of anger, self-pity, rage, resentment and one or two others - and did it several times.

In less than two minutes, our granddaughter went to grandma and wrapped her arms around her.

The devil doesn't play fair. He's quick to attack even young, defenseless children. But we don't have to let him get away with it. God's plan extends to children. Jesus told His disciples *(Matthew 19:14)* to suffer the little children to come to him. That's much better than letting them suffer!

THEATRICS

One day, Faye and I were holding a Bible study at a nearby nurs ing home. As Faye was teaching, one of the attending residents began speaking scriptures out loud. The scriptures were fine, but the timing wasn't. She was disrupting and distracting from the teaching of God's word.

Sitting in the meeting, I began to quietly bind any spirit I thought might be at work. The ill-placed scriptures kept on. Then I thought of rebuking a spirit of theatrics. Almost immediately, the nice lady quieted down and the teaching went on unhindered. The devil, of course, hates to hear the truth taught, because it can set his captives free. But, in the name of Jesus, any of his disturbing spirits has to cease and desist.

PAIN

Pain is not a normal defense mechanism of our bodies. It's demonic. Isaiah 53 tells us Jesus Christ bore our pains for us.

One of the teenagers in our church celebrated her sixteenth birthday at a local roller rink. Her family rented the rink and friends and relatives were invited.

As the young people, and a few adults, went whipping around the rink, we noticed a young lady on the sidelines looking quite sad. She had hurt her knee and couldn't skate on it. So she was spectating. Faye and I asked the young lady if we could pray for her. She agreed - and we cast out that spirit of pain. The happy astonishment was evident on the girl's face. She began to cry. Then, after God had taken pain from her, He was able to take her into His kingdom when the young lady asked Jesus Christ to come into her heart and be her Lord and Savior.

That's what a well-known Christian leader has called "power evangelism"!

Terry was dying from diabetes. Just in time, he received a kidney transplant. After the operation, his wife came out of intensive care and said to her waiting mother-in-law, "It's not right someone should be in such pain!" Terry's agony was excruciating.

But that was subject to change. Terry's mother, an active member of God's HMO, dashed into intensive care and took her authority. Putting one hand on Terry's head and another on a shoulder, she blurted out (as she recalls) "In the name of Jesus, Satan, I bind you, and I command you, spirit of pain, to come out!" The "shoo" sound that ensued was so noticeable that the nurse, who was leaning against the window sill, sat up. More importantly, the pain left Terry. He went into a peaceful sleep and during the rest of his stay, he experienced no further pain.

The Pain Extractor had taken over. And he's far more effective than any pain-killer can possibly be.

About fourteen years ago, our church was meeting in a hotel. One Wednesday, I was hurrying to arrive on time for the service. After parking the car, I strode quickly toward the entrance and banged head-on into a solid glass see-through front door of the hotel. My nose didn't break, but it could have.

What did happen when I walked into that door I thought was open? Nothing. How come? I immediately began refusing a spirit of pain in the name of Jesus. Believe me, I did it fast and furiously. After a minute, it was clear that there was no pain. I had felt the impact, but not any pain. I had refused it and it didn't surface.

It was a Sunday afternoon, and our family had gathered for dinner. A happy time. But our future son-in-law had pain in his body. He agreed to prayer. And when we commanded that spirit of pain to leave him, in the name of Jesus, it did. Pleasantly surprised, the young man, a Christian, was quick to witness to God's healing minutes later when the family had gathered at the dinner table. He was right on. Psalm 145:6 instructs us to speak of His awesome acts.

One night, as I was wending my way back to bed after visiting the bathroom, I rammed my right foot into a box on the bedroom floor. Ouch! But almost immediately, I began refusing any spirits of pain and inflammation in the name of Jesus. Over and over I did this - almost rapid-fire. Happily, after about two minutes, the pain which had begun strong was gone. And I could go back to sleep.

Like taking Vitamin C at the start of a cold, the sooner you call in God's health-care provision the better. If you let the enemy establish a beachhead, it may be more difficult to drive out the invader.

Extensive leaf-raking can be a pain - in the back. Admittedly, it's excellent exercise. But, after a couple of hours that includes bagging the multitude of leaves you've raked, your back could get a little achy. That's what happened to me at the large last leaf-roundup last autumn.

As my back began hurting, I started to feel sorry for myself. Then, I realized I could do something about the situation that I had been, stupidly, putting up with all fall. Finally, I began rebuking the spirit of pain in Jesus' name. Sure enough, after about five minutes, the pain took off and didn't come back.

If Jesus carried our pain on his back, why should we allow it on ours?

A few summers ago, I was painting the outside of our house. A batch of wasps was nestled in raftered areas. Despite spraying, one of them got through and stung me as I stood on the ladder. Then the real battle began. I began rebuking any spirits of pain, inflammation and swelling. As long as I kept using my authority, the pain subsided. When I slacked off, it came back. Finally, after two to three hours, there was little pain left on the finger where the wasp had stabbed me. The house painting could continue.

Angels are ministering spirits that God sends out to help those who are slated for salvation (*Hebrews 1:14*). That was evidenced in the back of our church about eight or nine years ago. Edna had pain in the area of her left elbow. She'd been entertaining it, on and off for months. On this occasion, we first commanded a spirit of pain to leave. Then we felt inflammation was involved, and we cast out spirits of inflammation and pain. After that, Edna felt better.

She also told us that after the commands were spoken in Jesus' name, she saw two angels "doing something" and she felt heat in her forearm and elbow. God, we believe, often uses angels as health-care carriers.

At a home meeting one night, Sandy, who had already experienced divine healing, told of something that had been hanging on. Seventeen years earlier, her back had been injured as a result of a car accident. She'd had the appropriate medical help, but a certain amount of pain would surface.

We began to pray - and rebuked to no avail. A compassionate Lord then gave us a word of knowledge informing us what to take authority over. It was a spirit of residual pain. When we commanded that spirit to leave, the pain Sandy was feeling at the time left. Here you can see the importance of addressing the precise spirit involved. If you're name were Tom Jones and someone called to Ben Smith, would you react?

Paul's back was hurting. After the Sunday service, he asked for help. Knowing that lower back pain is often caused by differing leg lengths, we first checked the length of his legs. (My wife is expert at this.) One was very slightly shorter than the other. Commanding a spirit of infirmity to leave his back and telling the back parts to come into proper alignment, we then commanded the shorter leg to grow out, all in the name of Jesus. As a result, Paul's back felt a little better. Laying hands on his back, we spoke to infirmity plus scoliosis - and nothing happened.

Not knowing what to do next, we prayed, and inflammation came to mind. So we cast that spirit out, along with pain and arthritis. Now, Paul bent over and noticed the pain was gone, his back felt much better.

We've learned from experience, and the Hunters, if you don't succeed, try again. And again. And again. If possible, don't give up until you see results.

Demonic attacks can occur at the most inconvenient times. One morning I was in my office at a downtown Chicago advertising agency. Another writer and I were having a conference.

As we were discussing, I suddenly started having chest pains. Although this was disconcerting, I did remember to take my authority in Jesus Christ and I began rebuking spirits mentally as the conversation continued. After two or three minutes, the pains stopped, and I could concentrate more fully on the meeting.

Anyone who's ever taken a commuter train with regularity knows there are occasions when a certain amount of sprinting may be necessary to make the train on time.

Late one afternoon, I was chugging along toward Chicago's Union Station - and going along with me were chest pains. Intent on making the train, I began rebuking the demonic attack in the name of Jesus. Primarily under my panting breath. And, as in the office, the pains disappeared. The happy ending is that I did make the train, where I sat down, wound down, and relaxed.

Those occurrences were over a dozen years ago. Since then, I've had no heart problems.

ARTHRITIS

Perhaps nothing can be more painful than arthritis. And yet the demons behind this crippling disease are quick to leave the premises when God's radiation moves in. Take the case of Diane.

This young lady is an adroit on-the-air-interviewer for a radio station in the East. After we had completed taping a phone interview, we asked Diane if she could use any prayer. At the time, she was preparing to leave for a period of duty in the reserves. It would be the usual camp-out, not-much-in-the way-of-amenities situation. To make the outlook even less inviting, Diane suffered from cervical arthritis with accompanying pain. She'd had it for years.

When that spirit was commanded to leave in the name of Jesus, Diane felt a coolness in her body.

Months later, we spoke to her again. Good news. She was feeling much better and had been since that day of taping.

God loves radio broadcasters. He's given them the talents they so often use so well. Consider Lisa, who is also the manager of a very unusual radio station in the South.

After our phone interview on "God Heals Today", Lisa disclosed a long-term knee problem that began when she fell at the city's convention center. After rising in the morning, she would limp around for the first part of the day because of the stiff knee. Throughout the day, she was in constant pain. When spirits of pain, swelling, inflammation and arthritis were cast out, Lisa felt the power of God on her body. Several months later, I called and checked with Lisa. She reported that God had, indeed, healed her knee. No more morning stiffness or any pain. Not only that, but He had also healed a swollen ankle she hadn't mentioned earlier. As His Word says, He is able to do more than we ask or even imagine He will do! (*Ephesians 3:20*) God hates arthritis and its buddies, no matter where they occur.

CANCER

And what's so unusual about Lisa's radio station? It has a call-in show that features staff members praying for the sick and casting out demons in the name of Jesus. As you might imagine, the show is very popular - and - it is highly effective.

One day, a lady called the station wanting prayer for her diagnosed case of cancer. No question that she had the dread disease or that she wanted to get rid of it. There was no question of what the show host would do, either. In the name of Jesus, she commanded that foul spirit of cancer to leave the caller. (*Ephesians 3:20*)

After her next checkup, the cancer-caller called back. To the surprise of her doctor, there was no longer any sign of cancer. The demonic spirit had been eliminated and God had healed her. That's what can happen when one of His HMO representatives swings into action. As happens so often, the healer and the HMO rep can be miles apart. Read Mark 7:26 and you'll discover that (about 1,967 years ago) Jesus cast a demon out of someone who was also in absentia. And, he's still doing it through His body on earth (the church) today.

In the case of Vicki, the Lord again demonstrated His name is above cancer and that disease is no match for it.

Vicki, at that time not yet thirty, had cancer of the uterus. This young mother, a strong believer, was quick to receive prayer. But, time went on and the tumor grew on. Then Vicki listened to a tape about David's victory over Goliath - and how David came against his demonic enemy in the name of God.

Encouraged by the content of that tape and familiar with her authority in the name of Jesus. She commanded the cancer to die.

In less than two weeks, after she began battling the cancer with the name of the Lord and the word of God, Vicki was a winner. The tumor left her. And after more than seven years, there has been no recurrence.

STROKE

Eleanor had just arrived at a local nursing home the day before our Bible study. She had suffered a stroke and was paralyzed on one side.

We asked her if she believed Jesus was ready to heal her. She responded, "I know He is!" And Jesus did for her according to her faith.

After we commanded a spirit of death to leave her in the name of Jesus and lay hands on her, she felt warmth and life moving into her leg. She was able to move it and later walk on it.

Why did we cast out a spirit of death? Because that side of her body was dead.

DEAFNESS

When it comes to audiology, no human specialist can compare with the one who set up the system in the first place. Not long ago, in a Midwestern city, a fourteen-year-old girl was brought into an evangelist's meeting. She came forward for prayer and God healed her. What was so unique about this healing was the girl's condition. She was profoundly deaf - never had heard a sound in her life. The change took place when God took over. That happened when the evangelist moved in his God-given authority . Placing hands on the girl's ears, he bound the deaf spirit and cast it out in the name of Jesus. Instantly, the girl's ears opened. She could hear the snap of a finger. She could hear the ticking of a wrist watch. She could hear the spoken word, "Jesus". And she repeated that wonderful name, the first word she had spoken in her life.

ALLERGIES

An out-of-state visitor came to a meeting of our home Bible fellowships. At prayer time, she requested help with allergies. For at least ten years, this very sweet lady had been burdened with a wide variety of allergies - including outdoor causes, clothing and food. "You name it, I've got it!" she declared.

A believing Christian, our visitor had been prayed for many times, but with little result. The Master Allergist was about to turn frustration into jubilation.

We commanded spirits of allergy to leave in the name of Jesus. And a strange thing happened. Out of the mouth of this gentle lady came a male voice. Three times it said, "Get out of here!" But we became more determined and kept commanding the spirit(s) to leave in Jesus' name. After a few minutes, the lady noticed a perceptible difference, she was feeling better. Her evil occupants had been moved out.

About two months later came the good report. The lady's allergist had discontinued all of the medication her patient had been taking. Everything had turned from positive to negative. She was gloriously healed from every allergy.

EPILEPSY/STUTTERING

During the course of talking to book stores regarding "God Heals Today", a very unusual opportunity for employing God's health care arose.

Speaking on the phone to a buyer in a distant book store, I realized the gentleman was stuttering heavily and uncontrollably. He told me he also had epilepsy. The epilepsy and stuttering had been affecting him for years.

Since he was open to prayer, I took authority over the spirit of epilepsy in the name of Jesus and commanded it to leave him. We went on talking, but something had changed. He had stopped stuttering! Completely.

Apparently, the epilepsy had caused not only his seizures, but his stuttering as well.

Under God's plan, epilepsy can be more than controlled, it can be eliminated, along with all of its ill effects.

LUST

Some years ago, I visited a downtown client to discuss a marketing project. My client was very bright and knowledgeable. And also an attractive female. As we were discussing pertinent information in her office, some improper thoughts came into my mind - literally from out of the blue. Knowing what to do, I quickly, under my breath, rebuked Satan, over and over. After a minute or less, those knocking thoughts were knocked out. They left completely. I had followed God's biblical injunction to take every thought captive to the obedience of Christ. (*II Corinthians 10:5*)

DIVORCE

Perhaps you've known a seemingly happily married couple of many years whose marriage suddenly ended in divorce. Maybe there seemed to be no reason for the split. Maybe there wasn't.

Consider what almost happened to Frances, a suburban wife whose marriage was not at all rocky. A good friend of hers divorced her husband and thoughts of divorcing her husband entered into Frances' mind. It might be fun to be single.

Since Frances was a Christian, she received counsel from a fellow Christian who sensed something wrong in what had now become a decision to move toward divorce. And that lady cast out a spirit of divorce from Frances.

After that, Frances realized she had a fine marriage. Her thinking turned around, become logical again. The desire for divorcing her husband left her. And her marriage was saved. The devil, who hates marriages and families, had come against her mental health. But divine laser surgery had plucked the log from her eye, so she could see the truth.

HOMOSEXUALITY

The young man we'll call Frank was fifteen years old. At the end of a Bible study Faye and I conducted at a home for youth, we asked who wanted prayer. Frank was one of those who did. He said he was a homosexual and didn't want to be.

This was a first-time situation for us, but Jesus did say in Luke 10:19 that He had given us authority over ALL the power of the enemy and nothing would harm us. So, in His name, we attacked the enemy stronghold. We began rebuking spirits of sodomy, homosexuality and others to leave that boy.

The spirits in him threw him to the floor - and he began thrashing around. For nearly fifteen minutes the battle went on and the spirits resisted. But finally, Jesus won again. The boy relaxed. The spirits had departed their from vessel. Frank voluntarily told us he felt different. And he was a happy young man.

Would those spirits try to reenter the boy? Most likely. Could he fend them off? Yes, if he bound and resisted them in the name of Jesus. And if he avoided places and people of temptation.

If anyone tells you homosexuality is merely another normal lifestyle, don't you believe it! To God, it will always be an abomination (*Leviticus 18:22*) and the act "an indecent act" *(Romans 1:27)*. God loves the individuals, but detests the sin.

DELUSION

Glenn was hearing voices. They weren't audible, but came into his mind.

As weeks went on, the voices began telling Glenn about his great future and he felt proud that God was revealing such wonderful information to him. For several months, Glenn carried a notebook and wrote down what he was told.

Finally, Glenn was told to lie down in the middle of one of his city's boulevards. He was also told to roll down a stairway. Even then, he still thought he was hearing from God. Of course, he wasn't.

One night, Glenn, a relatively new Christian, angrily strode out of a prayer meeting. He wasn't being appreciated. Experienced members of the prayer group realized Glenn was demonically-deluded and obsessed. And later in the meeting, they bound the devil in the name of Jesus Christ.

At the time of the binding, Glenn, at home, reports it was if scales

53

were removed from his eyes. A scripture came across his mind - "by their fruits you shall know them." *(Matthew 7:20 KJV)* And Glenn knew he had been demonically deceived. He also knew he needed help.

He walked to a living room bookcase where there was a book on deliverance. And he stood there for about an hour, until his wife (who was at the prayer meeting) came home.

The next day, friends who were well-versed in deliverance were called. That next weekend, God's mental health provision was invoked and caregivers began to apply it. Over a period of about two days, Jesus Christ set Glenn free, loosed from most of the spirits that bound him.

God's plan had been followed. The spirits had been bound earlier in the week, so they couldn't function. Then, on the weekend, with the help of words of knowledge from the Lord, spirits had been loosed, driven away, so Glenn could be loosed from their control.

SATANISM/SUICIDE

About ten years ago, one of the new employees of a Chicago-area church had a rare opportunity to experience 'the authority of the believer." A troubled man came to his office - he had a fear of committing suicide. The idea had been coming from voices that spoke to him.

Was this visitor insane? No, he was the high priest of a suburban satanic church. Demons had been directing his life, but he was balking at suicide.

The church worker was scared, almost paralyzed with fear. Did the man have a gun with him? He had never faced anything like this before. Even more frightening, his guest began to hiss like a snake.

Then the Christian began to use the name of Jesus Christ. Haltingly at first, but louder and louder, ever more vehemently, he took authority in that name.

After many minutes of commanding the spirits to leave, the battle ended. The satanic high priest slumped from his almost rigid position. He had been freed in the name of Jesus Christ. The devil deludes and destroys. God heals and saves - even His enemies.

THE OCCULT

Portability is an appealing feature of God's Health Care Plan. Christians can access it wherever they go - no matter how far from home.

Brad, a Chicago-area pastor, teacher and evangelist, was holding an outdoor meeting on the Philippine island of Cebu. As he spoke, his message was translated into Tagalog, the language of the country. Apart from the crowd, but listening, was a native witch doctor. After he finished preaching, Brad called for healing. The witch doctor was among those who moved forward. And it wasn't easy. His body was numb from his neck through his knees.

Vince began commanding occult spirits to leave the man. As he completed the deliverance, he lay hands on the witch doctor. The warm power of God began to flow down the exact area of numbness in the man's body. And he was healed - in a matter of moments.

In this case, the healing could occur only after the blocking spirits were driven out.

The end of the story was the beginning of a new life for the witch doctor. After experiencing the power of God that was greater than the power of Satan that he used, the man asked Jesus Christ to come into his heart and he became a born-again Christian.

His fickle former master had afflicted his own man. A compassionate God had delivered and healed him - and called him to Himself.

AND A GOOD DEAL MORE

Imagine, if you can, what it would be like to have an uncontrollable desire to rock - in other than a rocking chair.

A lady we'll call Judy who lived in the eastern part of the country had that awful problem. As if that weren't enough, she was a pacer and could scarcely stand still. Add to that an unusual way of nose-blowing that sounded like a foghorn, and you have a hurting human who got fired from job after job because she was a distracting irritant.

Judy saw many psychiatrists. Nothing helped. Until she started getting prayer in church - climaxing with the glorious day her pastor got angry at the devil and cast out "Satan, and all your cohorts, in the name of Jesus!" That's when God's mental illness expulsion plan kicked in. And demons were kicked out.

At last report, Judy had no further urges to rock, roll, pace or even sound like a foghorn. One member of the congregation told her. "Now I can come to church" with no more of those distractions.

Judy was very happy about her new freedom. Her family and friends are delighted. Wouldn't you be?

Pastor John McCall of Baltimore Christian Faith Center has a church known for the many miracles God effects there. Norma, who had heard the good news, knew that , surely, her son could use a miracle.

Her son was born with undescended testicles. After eighteen months, only surgery seem to be the answer.

Norma took the boy to the church. Pastor McCall told the devil and company to leave the child. And it happened. Literally. God's painless surgery healed the boy.

An overjoyed Norma returned her son to Johns Hopkins, where doctors with surprise and wonder confirmed the miracle.

The devil's marauders had moved into Thelma with a laundry list of diseases. Here are most of them with type and longevity..... Arthritis (50 years), Liver Condition (45 years), Dry Eyes (30 years), Burning Feet (15 years), Ear Eczema (11 years) and Insomnia (9 years). Plus diabetes for many years.

But the devil and his truckload of diseases are trespassers on a Christian and can be booted off the property. And that's exactly what happened.

Thelma came to a full gospel church where they knew what to do. The pastor commanded spirits of infirmity, sickness and disease to leave her in the name of Jesus.

What happened? A lot. At our last report, everything was gone, except for diabetes. But, even there, Thelma was down to half of her previous medication and her sugar level was normal. After years of demonic afflictions, Thelma went to the right place for God's extensive same-day surgery and He didn't spare the scalpel.

The Bible informs us Jesus healed "many who were ill with various diseases." (*Mark 1:34*) Thelma certainly qualified.

Since we're investigating God's multiple-disease operations, let's look at Irma. If you saw her walk into church, your heart would certainly have gone out to her. When she appeared she was close to a basket case. An ear imbalance caused her to move almost drunkenly. She was blind in one eye and she had severe back problems.

This physically-oppressed lady had been diabetic for eighteen years. For twenty-eight years, she'd been medicated for high blood pressure. Allergies had long been active. She was ingesting a total of twenty-one different medications at the time she visited church at what began as a relatively normal Wednesday night service. It would house an awesome work of God.

The pastor was a no-nonsense shepherd who had no doubts about where sickness and pain come from. And he quickly prepared the operating table. He cast out the demons that caused and perpetuated Irma's ailments. As he commanded their departure in the powerful name of Jesus, they had to evacuate, driven out by the Holy Spirit.

The upshot was a new life for Irma. God had healed over fifteen items. Irma could see clearly, walk uprightly, and smile broadly. No more insulin injections. No more blood pressure medication. No more allergies.

After years as a virtual invalid, Irma could work. And her earnings wouldn't be drained by a multitude of medications.

At last, Irma could bring flowers into her home. She could even wear a bouquet. Because her Father, the Divine Physician, is well able to save to the uttermost. (*Hebrews 7:25 KJV*)

God's health care coverage knows no age limits. The cost doesn't increase nor does the coverage decrease.

He proved this to us again at a recent nursing home Bible study. The teaching was about using the name of Jesus to stop enemy attacks. And the Lord was quick to confirm His word.

One elderly lady had pain in her body. She told us the doctor wasn't sure of the cause. But God knew. As we prayed, the idea of hernia came to mind. Is there really such a spirit? Well, after we told it, by name, to leave her, the lady reported the bulk of her bodily pain had departed. The same lady had a hand that was numb. After casting out appropriate spirits, including one of numbness, much flexibility returned to her hand.

Poor hearing afflicted a lady. But when the deaf spirit was cast out, her hearing improved to such an extent that she could hear and understand behind her back and at considerable distances.

Another lady was housing a spirit of pain. We told her to do something she had never done before - tell the spirit to leave her in the name of Jesus. She did it - God did it - and she was pleasantly surprised.

After we told the group what the Lord was doing, another lady came up to us. She had an immobile finger. God was quick to respond to her faith and healed it.

God's love knows no bounds. Neither does a Christian's Jesus-bought authority over the devil's ravaging forces. The Bible makes no bones about it. "The kingdom of heaven suffers violence, and violent men take it by force." *(Matthew 11:12)*

Nursing homes are loaded with captives - to sickness, pain and a broad spectrum of emotional problems. Just drop in one, look around, talk to a few people and you'll get the picture. They don't need your sympathy, they need your help. And God, through His HMO, is ready to be their ever-present help. *(Psalm 46:1)*

The Good News Church ministry reaches at least a dozen nursing at least once a month. Our monthly reports normally indicate 24 to 42 manifest healings. From one nursing home in a suburb of Chicago comes this report for October 8, 1994:

1. Pain in shoulder left. 2. Pain & stiffness in legs left. 3. Pain in leg left. 4. Eyesight improved. 5. Back pain healed. 6. Arm & leg grew out. 7. Pain in ankle left.

Should we take pride in that? No, just satisfaction - and gratitude to the Divine Physician Who does it when we take authority in the mighty name of Jesus Christ, The Healer.

Nursing home or your home, God has the most compassionate of all health-care plans. Not surprising when we remember that He is love. *(I John 4:16)*

End Waiting Around

" In my trouble, I cried to the Lord, and He answered me."
(Psalm 120:1)

Often, God's nick-of-time surgery takes more than a few minutes. But even then, it can be a happy combination of the emergency room and the operating room in one convenient place and time period.

Actually, in the case of Wanda, a variety of well-embedded malignancies had to be uprooted with intensive care.

Wanda had severe mental and emotional problems. She had been hospitalized. Then, one Sunday, she tried to kill herself. She failed - and was glad. But she wanted and needed help in a hurry.

So, that same morning, she went to a full gospel church in the lower Midwest. At the end of the service, the operation began - after the pastor dismissed anyone who wanted to leave. (Only about two dozen remained.)

The lady was loaded with demons. Her eyes peered out wildly. She began to foam at the mouth. Although she was a Christian, she had difficulty speaking the name of Jesus. Instead, deep, gutteral voices came from her. "You're not going to stop us!", one boasted. "We're going to kill her", another threatened.

But the name of Jesus in the mouth of a believer is more potent than the strongest radiation ever conceived. One by one, spirits were addressed by the pastor and his deliverance team. It was pinpoint surgery, zeroing in on each demon that was either evident or manifested. Although demonic threats, such as we noted above, came through the mouth of the victim, God's deliverers were undaunted during nearly two hours of battle.

The first trespasser ejected was a spirit of fear. Then, a suicide spirit was cast out. Next to leave was lust. Then drug addiction. Finally, infirmity.

At last, the operation was over. The highly harassed woman was set free. A great peace settled over her. And those in the operating room breathed a deep sigh of relief.

Wanda, driven to the brink of suicide, had been delivered from evil, as Christians, who knew their authority in Jesus Christ, weren't

59

afraid to use it.

Faye, our youngest son, and I were driving westward to visit one of our sons and his family. When we neared the Des Moines area, the devil attacked Faye with a vicious bladder infection. My wife seldom complains, but she was hurting. We stopped at a supermarket and picked up cranberry juice. And settled into a motel.

The next morning, Faye was about ready to go to an emergency room. But we decided to look first to our health care Provider. As Faye lay in bed, I lay a hand on her and she did the same, and we took authority over the invading spirits saying, "In the name of Jesus, infirmity, infection, cystitis, inflamation and pain - go!" We prayed in tongues, we quoted healing and authority scriptures - and kept it up.

After about an hour, the peace of God began to move in, and the pain began to move out. At the end of roughly ninety minutes, all of the pain was gone. Faye,who had been on the brink of screaming, was healed.

We then dressed, had breakfast, and drove on until we arrived at our son and daughter-in-law's home after dark that night. Never will we forget God's house call on that blessed day in June of 1994.

A team of specialists at a prestigious Southern hospital told Marilyn Spenner her son, John, would be permanently blind. He had a split optic nerve. No surgery, medication or glasses could improve his sight.

The blindness had come on the young man after extensive back surgery that cost close to $250,000.

As Marilyn prayed, she felt God wanted her to go right into intensive care and cast out that spirit of blindness.

Moving to John's bedside, Marilyn put spittle on his eyes, lay hands on them and commanded a spirit of blindness to leave him in the name of Jesus.

Very soon afterward, twelve physicians came by to check John's condition. To their surprise, he could see light. He could make out a doctor's hand. One physician held up two fingers. John told him he saw two fingers. The amazed doctors walked out in silence. The attending nurse told mother and son she had never seen anything like it .

In a matter of days, John could not only see in black and white, but in color as well.

Five years later, the "permanent blindness" continues to be permanently missing. John continues to see quite well.

Providentially, the world's most renowned health care provider had taken over in that intensive care ward. And He provided very intensive and complete eye care.

admire and women envy!

Billie had a different and more common kind of skin irritation. She had a rash on her body that was not going away. And since Billie was smart enough to attend a church that believed in receiving all the benefits of God's Health Care Plan, she was comfortable asking for healing prayer.

The staff members she spoke to lay hands on her and commanded the rash to go. Billie noticed no reaction. With questioning, she admitted she had been experiencing considerable fatigue for some time. With this new knowledge, the staffers commanded spirits of fatigue and chronic fatigue syndrome to leave Billie.

After dealing with the fatigue factor, the prayers then spoke again to the spirit causing the rash. Success! This time, Billie felt the heat of the Holy Spirit on her body. Something apparently was underway.

No more than a week later, Billie reported the rash had totally disappeared. That was also confirmed by her doctor. Oh, yes, she hadn't been getting as fatigued, either. Sometimes, there's more to a disease than we notice on the surface. God's diagnoses and procedures, of course, go more than skin deep.

Open Wide to Divine Dentistry

"My son, give attention to my words...For they are life to
those who find them, and health to all their whole body."
(Proverbs 4:20,22)

Consider the real surgery He performed on Sarah. This mother of six had experienced pain and headache. Her jaw and temples were affected. Her dentist told her she didn't have an abscessed tooth or gum infection - she had TMJ. And this inflammation of the hinge joint of her jaw had made eating, sleeping and just living very uncomfortable.

X-rays showed Sarah's bite was off. But, because of pregnancy at the time, extreme dental work was postponed. As she kept grinding her teeth, she went through two retainers in a month. Three years or braces followed by a retainer helped.

Then, all the symptoms came back. That's when Sarah turned to fellow Christians for prayer. And one night, over the phone, a member of her church commanded a spirit of TMJ to leave her in the name of Jesus Christ and she received prayer in that name.

Sarah noticed a warmth come over her face. She felt as if an unseen hand had come in and moved her jaw. (Part of her problem was underbite.) She felt different - better.

As a result, Sarah lost mouth, jaw and head pain. She could eat chew and bite easily.

Her health care Provider had healed her.

Tri-Geminal Neuralgia. Not exactly a household word. It's known to dentists, doctors and those who suffer from it - like Marion. This lady came in to the office of her Christian dentist in great pain. The disease was in the ganglia on the side of her face. In its eruptive stage, it coursed through her jaw and ear.

Marion had been carrying TGN around for years. It could be triggered by stress, by a wind hitting the area of her face, or if she were bumped. It didn't take much to set it off. And that day at the dentist's it was doing its thing. This was over ten years ago and one of the few treatments available was cutting the nerve at the base of the brain

But Marion's dentist had a better idea. He cast out, taking authority in the name of Jesus Christ. And Marion was startled at the result. The pain had left. Her dental health improved drastically.

Two experts in the field had cooperated in her healing. The first declared war on the devil. The Second brought quick victory.

At the end of the seventies, when I was a young Christian, my wife and I were receiving excellent teaching on faith. So, when I was attacked with the worst toothache of my fifty-five years, I phoned Faye from my office in the ad agency and we decided I would call on the power of the Lord instead of calling the dentist.

For about a day and a half, in the name of Jesus, I kept refusing the infirmity in my mouth. Over and over, under my breath, at my desk , I rebuked and repeated and personalized Isaiah 53:5 that by Jesus' stripes I was healed. Tempted to call the dentist, I hung on.

Then, in the afternoon of the second day, as I walked down Chicago's Rush Street during the lunch hour, the Holy Spirit dropped two scriptures into my mind. The first was Matthew 4:4, "Man shall not live on bread alone but on every word that proceeds from the mouth of God." The second was Isaiah 55:11, that God's word wouldn't return to Him void (or empty). I realized that I lived by the word of God and had spoken (over and over) the scripture that by Jesus stripes I was healed, and those words of God would not return to Him unfulfilled. A faith sandwich, so to speak, arose in my heart. Those two new scriptures were the bread and the one I had been using was the meat.

At around the same time the Holy Spirit gave me that gift of faith (I Corinthians 12:9), my wife asked for prayer at a local Women's Aglow prayer session. She didn't state my problem except that it was physical. One of the ladies told her that if it was a front tooth, God had healed it. (She received the gift of a word of knowledge according to I Corinthians 12:8.)

Sure enough, the next day, the toothache began to fade away quickly. Later my dentist found no cavity in the location of the toothache. God's Dental Plan had provided the care I needed when I needed it.

Put Back Problems Behind You

"O Lord, heal me, for my bones are in agony."
(Psalm 6:2) (NIV)

Many years ago, I made a very wrong move. Ready to cut the lawn, I went to the metal shed in our back yard. For some reason, I stood too far back from the shed which had a rather high front lip. Bending over, I tried to lift out the heavy lawnmower. And I pulled my back out.

From that time on, my back popped out painfully and easily. No longer did I lift heavy sacks of groceries. I opted out of moving furniture in the house. So, not only did I suffer, but so did my wife.

Tranquilizers helped somewhat after the painful pop-outs, but I seemed to acquire some kind of residual back pain.

I visited osteopaths whose treatments helped but couldn't solve the problem. Concerned, they x-rayed my back. Apparently, my back was so twisted that one of the doctors wrote "Wow" on the x-ray, which he showed me. Not exactly reassuring information. These very capable doctors also informed me that because of my back problem, my left leg was shorter than my right leg. On their recommendation, I put heel lifts on my left shoes. Now, I was in better shape, but there was residual low level of back pain. And , I wouldn't chance heavy lifting.

Years later, after I became a Christian, Faye and I were attending an evening Bible study in a local hotel. One night, those with pain were invited to come to the front for prayer. My wife elbowed me, I finally went forward.

The two meeting leaders had me sit in a chair, remove my shoes and hold my legs out. They discovered the left leg was shorter than the right.

Within three minutes after they prayed in the name of Jesus, my left leg had moved out to the same length as the right. My wife and many of the thirty-or-so people there observed it. When I stood up, I felt different. And, the lower back pain had gone. God had lengthened the leg after straightening my back.

Shortly afterwards, the heel lifts were ripped off my left shoes. Never

66

again has my back popped out. (And it's been over 14 years.) Now I can and do lift heavy items, including forty-pound bags and cartons of 148 paperback books.

It makes sense. Since God created us, He certainly would know how to manipulate our bones and skeletal systems.

As more knowledge of the truth gets out to hurting Christians, God is growing out an increasing number of legs and arms. Most commonly, as I understand, short limbs stem from back problems. Consider that close to half of the men over forty may have back problems, and you'll see we have a national epidemic! And the sad part of this is that God can turn that around if we'll do our part.

When the Israelites had the Red Sea in front of them and the Egyptians coming up behind them, Moses cried out to God. The divine response, chronicled in Exodus 14:15, 16, was "Why are you crying out to me? Tell the sons of Israel to go forward. And as for you, lift up your staff and stretch out your hand over the sea and divide it, and the sons of Israel shall go through the midst of the sea on dry land."

Notice that even at the Red Sea, God didn't function sovereignly. Before he moved, Moses had to take His word and follow His instructions.

It's the same way today. If we, too, use what God has given us, our rod of authority - the name of Jesus Christ - He will move for us just as he moved for Moses.

Since God grew out my left leg, Faye and I have seen many arms and legs do the same when we took authority in the name of Jesus. The results are usually immediate or a matter of very few minutes.

How do we do it? Normally, we first command any spirits of infirmity to leave the back. Sometimes a spirit scoliosis (curvature of the spine) must be cast out, we command nerves, muscles, tendons, vertebrae discs and ligaments to relax and come into proper length. Then we command the short leg to grow. All, of course, in the name of Jesus. Often, the short arm or leg will move out during the command to the back.

Very often, it seems, lower back pain indicates one leg is shorter than the other. Upper back pain is more likely to reveal one arm is shorter than the other. Comparative arm lengths can be determined by having a person stand or sit in a straight position, stretch them out wide sideward and then quickly bring them forward in front of the body until the open palms almost meet. Comparative leg lengths can be checked when the legs are held together with thumbs placed on the inside of the ankle bones and held straight out from the body - as the person sits back against the back of a chair. The same commands to the back should be given for either short leg or arm situations.

Now, hold it — you may say — what do you mean you speak to the back, the arm or the leg? What gives somebody the right to command not only spirits but parts of the body as well? The Bible does. Not only does Luke 10:19 give Christians authority over all demonic power, but John 14 and Psalm 8 are also applicable.

In John 14:13, Jesus promises, "And whatever you ask in My name, that will I do." But, in John 16:23, He says, "Truly, truly, I say to you, if you shall ask the Father for anything, He will give it to you, in My name."

Did you ever think it strange that in John 16, Jesus tells us to pray to the Father in His name, but in John 14, He tells us to ask Him?

The most fitting translation of that passage in John 14 becomes evident when you look up the Greek word used for "ask". According to a popular concordance, that word, "aiteo" is usually a demand of something that's due. That means that John 14:13 best translates "Whatever you demand in My name, that will I do." Now look at what precedes that, John 14:12. "Truly, truly, I say to you, he who believes in Me, the works I do shall he do also; and greater works than these shall he do, because I go to the Father." Because Jesus sits at the right hand of God, having given us authority in His name, He can and does perform by His Spirit, whatever we demand of any demons (who create all sickness and pain) and parts of the body that need straightening out due to accident, improper wear and tear, etc., including demonic infiltration with such spirits as arthritis, pain, swelling, inflammation, etc. We use His authority - He backs it.

Incidentally, but of importance, look closely at John 14:12 and notice Jesus does not say that His church, cumulatively, will do the works He did, but He says ANY BELIEVING MEMBER OF IT WILL DO THEM. Imagine what would happen to back problems if all Christians were out there "doing the stuff" as Charles and Frances Hunter might say. Most back problems would be a thing of the past. Billions would be saved in health care costs. Not to mention the time, trouble and pain of individuals and families.

Psalm 8 reveals the authority God gave His beloved mankind. Verse six states, "Thou dost make him to rule over the works of Thy hands; Thou hast put all things under his feet." We were made to rule, under God, over all things.

What's happened? Jesus Christ has restored to the people of God, the authority originally given them back in Genesis 1:26, when God gave man that dominion, and in Genesis 2:7, when He put him(Adam) in the garden of Eden to cultivate and care for it.

When Adam fell, it was, as the poet Milton has said , "Paradise Lost", and when Jesus Christ, (the second Adam) conquered the devil, death and hell, it was "Paradise Regained." Authority on earth has been returned to we mere men by our loving Father and our loving Savior.

Taking authority over other areas

Jessica was past middle age when she fell and broke her hip. She was told she could be crippled for life.

But she was open to prayer, even over the phone. The prayers commanded a spirit of infirmity to leave Jessica. Then they commanded her pelvis to come into proper alignment - all in the name of Jesus Christ.

Jessica states that her hip area began to rotate slowly and continued adjusting over a period of about twenty minutes. (She was standing and holding on at the time.)

Two days later, what had been constant pain was gone. Shortly after this, Jessica went for a scheduled check-up. The newly taken x-ray was compared with earlier ones. The doctor was amazed, he told Jessica she was almost healed.

A few weeks later, more x-rays proved Jessica was completely healed. Her doctor called it "unbelievable!"

God cares abut lesser pelvis problems, too. For close to five weeks, our oldest daughter had suffered stiffness getting out of bed in the morning. But the Heavenly Chiropractor was able to make the necessary adjustments.

In our kitchen, as our oldest daughter stood with her feet apart, her mother and I commanded a spirit of infirmity to leave and then told her pelvis to rotate into proper alignment. At the beginning, Faye also lightly lay hands on the back of our daughter's hips.

As we kept speaking the name of Jesus, and thanking the Lord, the Holy Spirit moved our daughter around, bending her in and out and swaying her. After about forty-five minutes, her body stopped moving. God had finished His work. The next morning, there was no more stiffness. Getting up was no longer a chore.

Years ago, a Russian who is now a cab driver in the Midwest, suffered damage to a little finger and thumb. Also a musician, he could no longer play the piano. Then, in 1994, an American evangelist who served in Russia and understood the language, happened to take his cab. He led the driver to receive Jesus Christ as Lord and learned about the hand.

Invited to the cab driver's home, the American, his wife and two local Christian friends, went to prayer. They took authority, in the name of Jesus, over anything that was causing the malformed digits. To the amazement of the Russian and his family, the finger and thumb straightened and grew out. To be sure of his miracle, the recipient of God's healing kept measuring his thumb and finger over and over.

Because of the boldness of His HMO, the Lord normalized the Russian's hand. After that happened, his wife and daughter, extremely impressed, became believers in Jesus Christ and were also baptized in the Holy Spirit.

This occurred on Thanksgiving night. And that apprreciative family could be thankful that God operates on holidays!

Philippians 2:10 promises that every knee shall bend at the name of Jesus. And that goes for every back, hip, and finger problem as well. As long as Christian caregivers will speak in His name.

Prune the Family Tree

"..visiting the iniquity of fathers on the children and on the grandchildren to the third and fourth generations."
(Exodus 34:7)

Loving parents and grandparents often leave inheritances. Wise guidance. A legacy of love. Sometimes, money.

But even the best of family trees can have a certain amount of infection that can get into the branches and cause harm. God's laser surgery can root out any unhealthy residue passed on from ancestors to descendants by generational spirits.

Joe had alcoholic parents. To say he was rejected and felt it is almost an understatement. As a result, he lived with the constant fear of being rejected again.

To protect himself, Joe worked hard and tried to please. As far as possible, he learned to control situations so there would be no unpleasant surprises. Unfortunately, this made him rather rigid, suspicious and domineering. It could be unpleasant for those affected by that spirit of control.

A Christian, Joe wanted to improve. So, he received help and lost some inherited spirits - including an inherited spirit of alcoholism, which was at the root of the other problems, including the desire to control. As a result of this deliverance, Joe became easier to live with.

Joe, like so many others, was stuck with inherited spirits, rejection, fear of rejection and others, passed down the family line. And - that spirit of alcoholism - which did not manifest as such in his life. He never was the least bit an alcoholic, but spirits kindred to alcohol showed up - and first, alcohol, then the others, had to be ejected.

More commonly, it seems, when a harmful spirit jumps from one generation to another, the spirit manifests itself directly in the offspring.

For example, during one of our nursing home visits, one of the residents asked for prayer for her sister, who had severe heart dis ease.

After we prayed for her sister (who was in another state), we rembered we had unsuccesfully prayed for the lady in front of us. We had commanded such a spirit of congestive heart disease to leave her, but nothing had transpired. Now - armed with the knowledge this could be an inherited spirit - we commanded an **inherited** spirit of congestive heart disease to leave the lady. And now something happened. She felt the warm power of God come over her heart area - and the symptoms began to recede.

As time went on, we discovered inherited spirits often were the culprits. In the case of arthritis, the spirits are quite often generational. And so, when we ineffectively tell arthritic spirits to leave, we then try inherited spirits and usually the pain goes immediately. Or, we will ask the party if the arthritis runs in the family before we take authority.

Sometimes, the Lord will divulge an inherited spirit to ministering Christians. One example occurred in our church. Those interested in praying for the sick at an upcoming special meeting had gathered for instructive training. One of them,Toby, had a painful right arm and wrist. "Inherited spirit of arthritis" came to the mind of a prayer. He immediately cast that spirit out in the name of Jesus. The pain and arthritis left and Toby and the group had learned a lesson from The Instructor.

A lady, mentioned in an earlier chapter, was freed from ten years of allergies. These allergies were inherited. Only after we commanded those inherited spirits to go was she set free. Now, whenever allergies are involved, we directly address inherited spirits.

Whether the inherited spirit is physical, mental or emotional (and we've come across anger, rejection and fear, to mention a few), God likes to cut us off from that kind of inheritance that's passed down (by demons) from one generation to another. Just because your dad and older brother died from heart disease, doesn't mean it has to happen to you.

Expect No Exceptions

"Today salvation has come to this house"

(Luke 19:9)

The Greek word for salvation in the above scripture is "soteria". It includes deliverance and health.

Today, God is healing families. Even his Major Medical provision covers households and extended family. Nothing is too overwhelming or insignificant to Him.

That's very evident when you observe His awesome care for the Wirth family.

For twenty one years, Margarette Wirth could do little for herself. She seldom spoke a word. The official diagnosis: Severe Mental Retardation. Margarette at twenty one couldn't have handled kindergarten. Her mother, Diane, had a full-time occupation caring for her daughter.

To make things worse, Margarette also had epilepsy. Seizures could be triggered by anything from a sore throat to a menstrual cycle. The medical community could do very little. The outlook was very bleak.

But God, whose every promise in the Bible is "yes" in Jesus Christ *(II Corinthians 1:20),* was ready to change the outlook. The health care He promises, He delivers.

My wife and I had learned something about Margarette through an activities volunteer at a nursing home. And we called Margarette's mother, Diane, a very devout Christian lady. After seeing God move mightily before and knowing of the remarkable miracles He wrought in the Bossmin and Williams families (see Chapter 16), we were ready to do what any believer can do.

As Diane joined her faith with ours, we (on the phone) commanded a spirit of epilepsy and spirits of gran and petit mal to leave Margarette in the name of Jesus Christ.

Margarette had been partially deaf for twenty years. So we spoke to the spirit of deafness and prayed for healing.

And there was more. Margarette also had cerebral palsy and walked unsteadily. In this case, we again spoke to "the mountain" and commanded the spirit of cerebral palsy to come out of her.

Then we did what Lydia Bossmin and Patti Williams had done for their children (see Chapter 16). As Diane lay hands on her daughter, we commanded a new brain into Margarette in the name of Jesus. And we thanked God for it.

Almost immediately, Diane reported, her daughter had responded, had felt something. And she picked up a section of a nearby Sunday newspaper.

Next, we learned that Diane's husband, Walter, had been experiencing pain since a 1966 operation had replaced six damaged disks in his spine, plus a neckbone and tailbone.

We cast out any spirits of infirmity, arthritis and others that seemed pertinent. Also we spoke to parts of the back to align properly. At the time, Walter felt something happen in his back.

Diane had been suffering from a cyst in her uterus for some time. Nothing was dissolving it. We commanded a spirit of infirmity to leave her uterus and cursed the cyst in the name of Jesus. Diane felt heat come over that area. And the pain left.

Here's what God did

We talked to Diane about two months later. Margarette had no more seizures. Minor infections that used to trigger them before came and went. For years, she had spoken only an occasional single word. Since the telephone session, Margarette had uttered her first sentence. She told her mother, "I want a bath." When one parent said "God bless you," to the other parent who had sneezed, the daughter also said "God bless you."

Diane reported her daughter has "gotten very smart." She now had curiosity and become interested in the newspaper - learning to read out loud with the help of her mother. Instead of wanting to lie listlessly in her pajamas all morning, Margarette had become eager to get dressed. She was also more interested in personal care.

Oh, yes. Her auditory problem was healed. She could hear well. And she could walk well. No more cerebral palsy.

Her father, a master electrician, no longer had back pain and continual aching. Before the prayer, he had been taking Darvacette each work day for pain. He was able to stop taking it. He had also become able to bend over farther and do more around the house.

Her mother, according to her surprised doctor, no longer has that ovarian cyst. That makes it easier for her to care for her rapidly-advancing daughter.

At the time of her good report, Diane was hurting in an achilles heel tendon. It was affecting her walking. We commanded a spirit of infirmity and any achilles heel tendon spirit out in the name of Jesus. She felt heat and noticed the pain had left. "I can stand on it", she announced.

How can words describe the love of God? Also mind boggling is the fact that He's ready and waiting to operate at the words of any believing born-again Christian. It doesn't have to be Oral Roberts or Benny Hinn. It could be you.

Now let's look at another family restored to better health as God's health care policy paid off again.

Ricardo lives in the Chicago area. He had been experiencing dizziness getting out of bed in the morning and on and off during the day. Medication wasn't handling the situation. Ricardo asked for prayer.

We lay hands on him and commanded any spirits of stupor and dizziness to leave him in the name of Jesus.

Some weeks later, Ricardo happily reported he was totally free of dizziness. he asked prayer for his wife who had been troubled with leg pain for seven years.

One Saturday evening we called Ricardo's home to pray for his wife. What ensued were remarkable works of God.

To begin with, we discovered Ricardo still had physical problems. He had long suffered from migraine headaches. His doctor told him the cause was the close proximity of two nerves to each other in the back of his head. When he became excited, angry, sad, etc., the migraines kicked in. Ricardo was medicated with haldol to help keep him from getting as emotional. But, he still would get headaches. There was head pain at the time.

Ricardo had felt inadequate at times, so we first cast out that spirit. Then, since he had been under considerable stress, we commanded that spirit to leave him. The headache diminished. Tension was cast out and there was further improvement. Next, we spoke to a spirit of migraine. Finally, we commanded the two nerves in his head to separate to a proper interval. The headache now left entirely. And when Ricardo pressed the part of his head which normally hurt with pressure, he said there was no pain there, either.

Ricardo's wife had been shot many years earlier, before she came to the United States. The wound had become infected, a certain amount of poison remained and there was pain in that right leg. Not much fun when you're employed as a housekeeper.

When we commanded a spirit of poison to leave her, most of the leg pain left. Then arthritis was driven out, again in Jesus' name. More improvement, Then spirits of pain and inflammation were ejected. The leg pain now was gone. And there was joy in that home.

But there was more to come. Ricardo's youngest son, a teenager, had been diagnosed with sickle cell anemia. This problem sometimes affected the active young man. When we commanded the spirit of sickle cell anemia to leave him, the boy felt warmth in his body. Subsequent testing showed he no longer had sickle cell anemia.

Ricardo's cousin was visiting during our call that night. Her malady was a vaginal infection of six years duration. After taking authority in the name of Jesus, all of the pain she had been experiencing at the time left her.

The divine Family Doctor had healed four people in one family in less than two hours. As Jesus has promised, in John 14:13, that whatever we demanded in His name He would do "that the Father may be glorified in the Son."

And that Saturday night, He did it.

Bone Up On Cutting It Out

"Nor is there any health in my bones"
(Psalm 38:3 NKJV)

One of the most common, painful and crippling diseases around is arthritis. Osteoarthritis, Rheumatoid Arthritis, Gout, and more. Whatever the type , it's a big pain.

In 1994, the Arthritis Foundation reported that about thirty-seven million Americans are suffering from this inflammatory disease, which is usually chronic. One in every three families is affected by it. Even though research is ongoing, there is still no known cure or total long-term relief.

Arthritis, like every other disease, is demonic. We discover it and cast it out in nursing home after nursing home - and elsewhere. Based on our experience, no physical sickness is more prevalent among the elderly residents. Many of their hands are gnarled. Their bones ache. Their backs are bent in pain. Our hearts go out to these sufferers. And we get great satisfaction in finding how easily these spirits depart from their victims in the name of Jesus, taking pain with them.

Although arthritis is usually easy to drive out, it often tries to return quickly. To offset this, we teach arthritic afflictees how to rebuke the spirit for themselves. Many have done this and experienced the end of recurring pain.

This was the case with an elderly lady, around eighty, who had arthritis. Very often, when we'd visit the nursing home, she'd be suffering, and we'd cast arthritis out - with success. And it would come back on her. Again and again. So, visit after visit we'd again cast it out.

After months of this, we automatically asked the lady if she'd like prayer against the arthritis. To our surprise, she said "No." She was rebuking that spirit itself, and it would leave her! She seemed more cheerful and looked better. Faye and I were thrilled that she was taking her authority and the Lord was, of course, confirming His word.

Our nursing home experience (and what we've learned from oth-

Look Below the Surface

"His flesh shall be fresher than a child's"
(Job 33:25 KJV)

The same God Who freed Job from a horrible skin condition, is quite capable of doing the same for any of His people today.

Jackie Lahey had warts - ugly warts - on her hands and knees. They first appeared in early childhood and increased until they became an embarassment. Her mother remembers how Jackie came home from grade school with tears in her eyes. Some of her friends weren't allowed to play with her anymore. The warts, their parents feared, could be contagious.

Frustrated, Jackie's mother took the girl to a physician who started her on medication that proved completely ineffective. Not only did the warts remain, they proliferated. By 1979,when Jackie was in the eighth grade, the warts covered her hands and knees - in clusters of three and four.

At this point, Jackie's mother, a born-again Christian, turned to her miracle-believing pastor. He and his wife invited her to their home to hear a tape testimony of someone whose daughter had suffered from more than forty warts covering her arms and hands. Jackie heard the girl's father relate how he commanded the growths to leave his daughter in the name of Jesus Christ. He told of the miracle that followed. By six weeks, the girl was free from every wart.

Emboldened by the tape testimony, Jackie's mother went home and waited for her daughter to return from school. Then she went into action. As she recalls, she said "In the name of Jesus Christ, I cast out these warts. They can't stay. I curse them from the roots." Then, through the days that followed, mother and daughter kept thanking God for removing the warts, even though there was no sign of it.

But - within two weeks - every one of the more than thirty warts had left Jackie's body. There were no scars, either. God had miraculously healed the girl - just as she was preparing to enter high school.

In the fifteen years since then, not one wart has returned. And at this writing , Jackie is a beautiful woman with the kind of skin men

62

ers) revealed something else. There is a common blocker that can keep the arthritic spirit around and prevent its loosing. **Unforgiveness.** Perhaps many nursing home residents have never forgiven whoever consigned them to the care facility. Perhaps they've held a grudge against another resident. In any event, we've found that when a resident wasn't getting loosed from arthritis, the reason was often unforgiveness. When that person does forgive, and asks God to forgive them for holding it, God will usually drive out the spirit quickly when it's commanded to go. Sometimes, the arthritic pain will leave immediately following the forgiving. As Jesus teaches in Mark 11:25 "...and whenever you stand praying, forgive, if you have anything against anyone; so that your Father also who is in heaven may forgive you your transgressions." Unforgiveness is sin and puts the unforgiver in the devil's territory and allows that spirit to stay.

Another open door for arthritis is **injury**. We have often prayed for people who have been injured - in a car accident, a fall, etc. Often the pain wouldn't leave as we thought it should.

Then we discovered arthritis was involved. The party may have never had arthritis before. No matter. He or she had it now.

Recently, we learned that the insurance industry is well aware of the arthritis-after-injury relationship. A friend of ours is a claims representative for a large insurance company. And he's been told, in case of an accident, to factor into the financial settlement, an amount for potential arthritis. This, he commented, is a common industry practice.

Arthritis. Any way it comes or clings, it goes in the name of Jesus. To those enrolled in God's Health Care Plan, there are no incurable diseases!

How to File and Get Approval

"You will also decree a thing , and it will be established for you"
(Job 22:27)

God's primary desire is for our entire person - spirit, soul (mind, emotions and will) and body "be preserved complete" *(I Thessalonians 5:23).*

It's not unscriptural, then, that God sometimes goes beyond healing afflicted parts of us. He Who said ,"Behold, I make all things new" (Revelations 21:5 KJV), is willing to do just that, when we have the need and the faith for it.

A classic example is the following highly-documented, true story of our Provider's miraculous supply from his far-more-than-prosthetics department. It is reprinted from the book, "God Heals Today", and then updated.

Tina Bossmin

By the age of three, Tina Bossmin hadn't spoken a word. Suspecting their daughter might be deaf, her parents took her to Braun Center in the Chicago suburbs. It was early 1987.

The diagnosis of two psychologists and a speech therapist shocked the Bossmins - Tina was autistic and slightly retarded. She wasn't speaking because she was withdrawn and shunned love and affection, symptoms of an autistic child.

The Bossmins placed Tina in First Orland Center, a school for the handicapped. Later, she was transferred to Doctor School.

Determined to help her daughter, Lydia Bossmin attended a school in divine healing at Midwest Christian Center.

Encouraged by what she'd learned, Tina's mother was ready to act. In the morning of October 24th, Lydia placed her hands on Tina's head and commanded a new brain with above normal intelligence into her daughter in the name of Jesus Christ. Then she sent the child to school. That afternoon, when Tina came home, she noticed a balloon hanging in the house. And she said "Oh, look a balloon!"

These were the first words she had ever spoken.

Lydia was thrilled. Her thirteen-year-old son "nearly flipped." Then she read from the daily report sent home by Tina's teacher. Tina had had an excellent day - and "for the first time she responded to two-sentence commands."

Tina's improvement was rapid. By the end of the school year, she was judged to be advancing rapidly. At four-and-a-half, Tina was talking freely, responding to people with interest and affection. She had so completely changed that Doctor School referred to her as "the miracle child." Her teacher stated that Tina no longer required full-time special education and should be placed in a regular pre-school class.

How about the mental retardation? In that same year, Tina tested at the academic level of a six-year-old.

In an October, 1992, meeting with the diagnostician, speech therapist and counselor, Tina was pronounced no longer needing any extra help in speech and other areas.

In her final testings, she tested "above normal" in math and and intelligence, (an answer to her mother's prayer) the only tests given her. She has now been released from all special education teaching.

In December, 1992, Tina celebrated her ninth birthday. An honor student, she has also had a perfect attendance record for more than two years.

Because her born-again Christian mother learned her authority in the name of Jesus Christ -and used it, God has completely freed Tina Bossmin from the dark prison of autism and the bonds of retardation.

Here's the update on that story, originally published in 1993.

Tina Bossmin celebrated her eleventh birthday in December of 1994. And, Tina seems to be getting ever brighter. She has been chosen to participate in a special linguistics class after school. (Remember, this is the child who couldn't speak a single word less than eight years earlier.) She participated in the school play. And she has been honored with the Blue Bonnet Award after reading and reporting on twenty books, (a feat she accomplished in two months).

Tina continues on the honor roll and her attendance is very honorable. She hasn't missed a day of school in five years.

When her mother filed that claim for a new brain with above-normal intelligence, the Creator proved He's no piker and truly " a rewarder of those who seek Him." *(Hebrews 11:6)*

Another enlightening example of God's love and creativity is the following, copiously documented and confirmed story of our Provider's miraculous supply from His far-more-than-prosthetics Heavenly Depot. This case, also reported in "God Heals Today" and updated here, was possible, in part, because the good news about Tina Bossmin was told to Patti Williams.

Michael Williams

1991 was a very bad year for the Williams family. Their second son, three-year-old Michael, seemed like a hopeless case. Some experts from the University of Iowa suggested his parents consider putting him into out-of-home placement. Michael was virtually impossible to live with.

Diagnosed with brain atrophy and epilepsy, obviously retarded, Michael was also born with a malformed skull.

He had the intelligence of a ten-month-old and a personality only a parent could love. Angry and frustrated, Michael would not only get into tantrums, but was masochistic and would beat his head against anything that was handy. His crib had to be padded. Both of his parents are teachers and they searched every possible avenue of help. They dreaded placing the boy out of their home. But he required constant attention and seemed to have no future.

Then, when darkness surrounded the family, in the early months of 1992, Michael's mother heard of and decided to pursue divine healing through Jesus Christ.

She absorbed a video tape about a Christian's right to healing. She began to believe strongly that Jesus Christ would heal her child.

Taking action, Michael's mother brought her son to the Chicago area for hands-on prayer from friends who had experienced and believed wholeheartedly in divine healing.

For many hours, Michael received prayer, but results seemed to be minimal. Then one of the praying friends felt impressed to start speaking healing scriptures. And steadily, for perhaps twenty minutes,

Michael's mother and the two friends kept thanking God that by Jesus' scourging, Michael was healed. Faith seemed to rise in the room.

At this point, Michael's mother determined to take action again. She had been told of another mother who had commanded a new brain into her autistic child in the name of Jesus Christ - with miraculous results. (See the preceding Bossmin testimony.) And she decided to do the same thing.

Dashing to Michael's crib, his mother laid hands on her son and commanded a new brain into the boy in the name of Jesus Christ. Nothing, at that moment, seemed to happen. Yet, mother and friends began thanking God for Michael's new brain. They spoke over and over and over the Biblical promise (II Timothy 1) that Michael had a sound mind. Then, mother and son returned to Iowa City.

Less than three days later, the praying friends in Chicago received a phone call from an ecstatic mother. Something had happened to Michael. He was beginning to show a new awareness. And - the very shape of his head had changed! - a fact noted by Michael's father who had been skeptical.

In the next few weeks, Michael, the fearful introvert, began moving out, exploring things. He had become curious. He entered a new stage of understanding. Now, when he beat his head against an object, he cried. Realizing what he was doing, he stopped doing it. He became more patient, wanting also to please as never before. His attention span was lengthening dramatically.

A few months later, Michael went to the hospital for another brain wave test. For the first time, such an EEG was normal, not a trace of trouble showed. And, even Michael's neurologist stated that the shape of the boy's head had changed, indicating brain growth.

Now, at the age of four, Michael is getting glowing progress reports from his special school. His neurologist plans to withdraw him from medication. He is communicating for the first time, via words and signs. And his parents continue to thank Jesus for Michael's sound mind - deeply appreciative of the miracle the Lord has already brought about in their once-hopeless son.

Here's the update. At the end of 1994, Michael's progress continues. Completely off tegritol, he moves ahead. The boy, who at 3 1/2 was at the mental and emotional stage of a 10-month-old, is at this writing, in kindergarten during half of his school day. He has recently celebrated his sixth birthday. (And his birthdays, like Christ-mases, have now become joyful celebrations in the Williams house-hold.)

Around mid-1994, Michael's mother consulted with the neurologist about her son. She asked him for a prognosis for Michael's future growth. His answer was clear and concise. "He looked me squarely in the eye," relates Patti Williams, and said, "The sky's the limit." He also stated he no longer needed to see the boy. Already, Michael's special education teacher has called him "a quick learner" and has moved him into more academic studies.

Almighty God has given Michael "a future and a hope." *(Jeremiah 29:11)*

Michael's miracle is an exciting example of Mark 11:22-24 coming to pass. The fig tree cursed by Jesus has died. Jesus' first words in reply to Peter's comment are "Have faith in God ."(literally, "Have the faith of God") The faith of God is evident in Genesis 1 when He spoke and called things that were not into existence. Romans 4:17 tells us God "calls into being that which does not exist." In Mark 11, Jesus told his apostles (and us) to have that kind of faith. He also said that whoever speaks to a mountain and "does not doubt in his heart, but believes that what he says is going to happen, it shall be granted him."

When Patti Williams dashed to Michael's crib, lay hands on her son and commanded a new brain into him in the name of Jesus Christ, her faith was high, (after speaking God's word on healing for about twenty minutes), and at that moment she believed what she said would happen. At that point, she was meeting the requirements in Mark 11:23.

Jesus, in Mark 11:24, stated, "Therefore I say to you, all things for which you pray and ask (the Greek word for ask is here better trans-lated "demand"), believe that you have received them, and they shall be granted to you."

After Patti Williams commanded the new brain into her son (be-lieving it would happen), she then built her faith to believe she had received by speaking over and over for many minutes, the applicable part of II Timothy 1:7 - that Michael now had "a sound mind."(KJV) - and thanking God for it. She continued to speak the scripture and thank God during her return to Iowa City and for some time after that.

Less than three days later, God granted her desire and Michael had the new brain, attested to by the testing that showed no seizure activity (the EEG indicated normal brain activity). Other indications include Michael's remarkable new curiosity - and the neurolgist's statement that the shape of Michael's head had changed.

Patti Williams, without realizing it, had literally acted according to Mark 11:22-24. She had also fulfilled the principle enunciated in Romans 10:10 of believing in the heart and confessing with the mouth to effect salvation. (Remember, the Greek word for salvation includes health.)

Michael's mother had filed her claim according to her written contract with God. And God had approved it and fulfilled it.

Judy Thilly

God's Claims Department works for adults as well as children. Judy Thilly, a warm and friendly middle-aged lady, had hypoglycemia (the opposite of diabetes). She couldn't eat carbohydrates, because her body would turn them into sugar. She did eat more protein, including meats and cheese. But she didn't become hungry and lost weight.

Judy wanted healing. Her Health Care Provider wanted to give her even more. When she went forward for prayer at a major charismatic meeting in downtown Chicago, she told her situation to one of the ministering evangelists. Laying hands on Judy, the evangelist , in the name of Jesus Christ, spoke a new pancreas into her body.

On the way home, Judy commented to her husband that she was hungry - later she enjoyed eating carbohydrates. Yet, there were no adverse effects. In fact, when she went back to her doctor, her blood sugar was normal. Within three weeks after that, her cholesterol had dropped significantly and even her blood pressure had normalized.

That happened in the mid-eighties. In the mid-nineties, Judy has still experienced no further hypoglycemic problem. God had reached into his medical and surgical supplies and provided her with a new pancreas.

Certainly, He is El Shaddei, the God who is more than enough - and He has more than enough in his divine reserves to fulfill all of our claims.

Pray to Pinpoint the Problem

"And to another (is given) the word of knowledge
according to the same Spirit"
(I Corinthians 12:8).

How can you address a problem if you don't know what it is? Often, there's more to a healing of any sort than meets the eye, or the ear. But, we can be reassured, for God is not only our healer and deliverer, He is also our diagnostician. He knows everything. And He seems willing to pass a bit of that knowledge along to His people when and as the occasion demands.

Case in point: at one of our home Bible fellowship meetings, a man was suffering from a long-standing and painful back problem.We took authority over every possible culprit we could think of, but he received no relief. Then we got smart. And we asked God to show us the specific spirit, so we could cast it out. As we prayed in tongues, God graciously answered us. The word "lumbago" dropped into the mind of one of the attendees. Then, we cast out a spirit of lumbago and the pain left the afflicted man and we rejoiced with him.

Before another home meeting (also sponsored by our church), I was praying, and the Lord gave me a picture of a split fingernail on a thumb. During the meeting that followed, I asked if anyone had a problem with a finger. Sure enough, a middle-aged lady we'll call Jeannine said she had a split fingernail on one thumb, and it hurt. She hadn't told anyone, not even her husband, about it. But, of course, God knew and wanted to heal it.

So, we prayed and God took away the pain and healed the thumb., And, as sometimes happens, the Lord added another benefit. Jeannine had a poor relationship with her father and so she had difficulty looking on God as a loving , caring Heavenly Father. But, when she realized He cared enough about her to reveal and heal even a split fingernail, she realized how much He loves and cares for her.

No hurt is too insignificant to God. Healing us totally is part of God's Health Care Plan!

Jeff, who had read "God Heals Today", called from another state. He was having a problem with obesity. Yet, he was watching his intake, ate properly and didn't overeat.

He was frustrated and embarassed. As I prayed, the idea of a "glandular disorder" came to mind. Jeff didn't think he had any such problem. But a "spirit of glandular disorder" was spoken to. Jeff reported feeling the power of God come on his body, which was, I believe, the beginning of healing.

Also in the food and weight department, is the case of Leslie. She had, of necessity, been eating between meals to build herself up. However, after she was back to normal, she continued that kind of supplementary eating. She was unable to stop. And she asked Faye and I for prayer. It was obvious to Faye she had been and was under stress. But the idea of self-pity also came to mind, rather strongly. And Leslie admitted, she had been feeling sorry for herself.

So, we cast out self-pity as well as stress. And Leslie noticed a difference. Then, with those blockers gone, we commanded a spirit of gluttony to leave. And it did. To such an extent, that Leslie felt like something had been pulled out of her. In the days that followed, she's been able to control her eating. The constant desire to eat is gone. God is a very effective habit-breaker.

At a meeting of our church nursing home ministry staff, we prayed for one of the workers who had a heavy sinus infection. Nothing happened, until God revealed to another lady there was a residual spirit of nicotine involved.The lady had once been a smoker.

When that spirit was cast out, the Lord then healed the sinus problem.

God had again helped by providing a word of knowledge, one of the nine spiritual gifts noted in I Corinthians 12. Are these only for special, big name people? Of course not. Our health care Provider is very practical, He'll use whatever vessels are available. And he knows the importance of x-rays before operations.

Shed Those Scales

"And thus you invalidated the word of God
for the sake of your tradition"

(Matthew 15:6)

Remember that familiar song from the hit musical, "Fiddler on the Roof" titled "Tradition"? It took Tevye, the patriarchal milkman, a multitude of scenes, songs and a few atrocities to at least partly shake off some hindering aspects of the traditions he had grown up with.

Back in the days when Jesus spoke with authority and cast out demons, some Jewish leaders claimed he was doing it by the power of Satan. They were envious and legalistic. But, you can be sure Mary Magdalene appreciated being loosed by the Lord of seven demons. It allowed her to follow Him so fully that she was the first one He appeared to after He rose from the dead.

Then there was the Gadarene demoniac, who was delivered by the Lord from a legion of demons and put back into his right mind. He became a very effective witness to Jesus and gave his testimony in ten cities. He can be glad he didn't say, "Hey, Jesus, don't you think casting out a legion of demons is rather extreme and not keeping with the way the establishment has been (or not doing) deliverance?"

I know what it's like to be bound by tradition. And when I was blinded by it, I didn't realize it. As a faithful member of my church, I believed everything it taught me. And I was suspicious of anything opposed to what I was raised to believe.

Even after I became born-again (which my church had never informed me about), I did develop a new appreciation for people in other denominations. But I was still tied to my denomination's traditions.

Then, one night, God moved in a weekly Bible study my wife and I attended. (Actually, it was a mini-service, but if they had called it that, we might not have gone.)

After the teaching on the traditions of men, there was a call for anyone interested in getting free from tradition to come forward for prayer. Interestingly enough, close to half of the fifty or so in attendance went to the front of the room.

By this time, my wife and I had , over the weeks, seen great answers to prayer in those meetings. It was there that God grew out my left leg. So - eager for all that God had for us, we joined the prayer line.

As the two who were ministering came down the line laying hands on people, they reached a point about two away from me. No one had to touch me - only God. I felt a strong release in my gut and had an eyes-open vision. A pious-looking little demon with one large eye and feet that were slippers went tiptoeing across the screen and off of it.

Once that spirit of religious tradition that had blinded me was removed, the Holy Spirit began to show me, primarily in the Bible, some things that were wrong with the traditional teaching I had been encrusted with. The eyes of my understanding were opened *(Ephesians 1:18)*. And I could move forward more freely and fully in the Christian life.

As part of that new freedom of understanding, Faye and I joined a born-again, Spirit-filled, full-gospel church that believes that divine healing and deliverance is for today and for everyone, just as being born-again is for everyone. And the Lord has been able to use these imperfect vessels to help others grasp the truth - enjoy more of the abundant life Jesus promises - and help free other people.

For example, a gentleman in one of the southern states wrote and called me after seeing an interview on television. He had come from a different religious background than I, but his old denomination was suspicious of divine healing. Happily, he was breaking free. His eyes were being opened and our testimonies helped open them further.

He, like so many Christians, had not been aware of certain of his entitlements under God's Health Care Plan. If you're at all shackled by unbiblical traditions, consider praying according to Ephesians 1:18 & 19, that God will open the eyes of your understanding that you may know "What is the surpassing greatness of His power toward those of us who believe."

Also, you might look closely and prayerfully at Jesus' words in John 4:24 - "God is spirit, and those who worship Him must worship in spirit and truth."

Don't Lose Your Benefits

"Resist the devil and he will flee from you."

(James 4:7)

Why do some people healed by God lose their healings? That's a commonly asked question.

Reoccurrence happens because the same devil that lay the sickness, fear, depression, whatever , on a person has come back and done it again. In Luke 11:24 (NIV), Jesus warns us "When the evil spirit comes out of a man, it goes through arid places seeking rest and does not find it. Then it says, 'I will return to the house I left.'"

Louise lives in scenic Colorado. Unfortunately, her heavy load of allergies marred her landscape until they were cast out and she was totally freed.

However, about four years later, she was once again attacked with allergies. Rather than starting shots again, Louise called on God's Health Care Plan, and by herself, she fought off those spirits of allergy. She refused them in the name of Jesus. For several days she kept it up. And she won. The allergic attack ceased and Louise was fine. She knew God's provision against recurring illness and entered into it.

At a recent home meeting, Mara was bothered by nasal and sinus problems, basically caused by allergies. God had previously healed her.

Mara is a pleasure to pray for because she's always ready to receive from God. She's a lady of faith. But, when we lay hands on her and commanded the spirits causing the problem to leave, they didn't go. Questioning revealed that Mara had become fatigued. She admitted she had been pushing herself too hard, a great temptation when you have four small children at home. She confessed this as a sin. Then, we cast out a spirit of fatigue. She felt a release and was ready for the next stage.

With fatigue handled, we again lay hands on Mara and commanded such spirits as sinusitis, allergic rhinitis, bronchial asthma and others to leave in the name of Jesus. The pressure in her head began to ease, the clogged sinuses started to clear and Mara began to feel better.

The next morning she was greatly improved. And now she's more aware of the danger of getting overly tired and opening the door for the spirit of fatigue and a return of those physical enemies.

Incidentally, Mara has learned well to refuse allergic spirits and others when they try to get back on her.

Based on the more than twenty nursing homes our church has visited over the years, the most prevalent physical afflictions seem to be arthritis, pain and deafness. And, we get great satisfaction in helping Jesus drive off those spirits. Sad to say, in many cases, the spirits return and even two weeks later, residents are again talking about "my arthritis." Or, their hearing has returned to the state it was at before God healed them.

When you consider the minimal teaching the stricken residents have received and the medically-oriented nature of nursing homes, you can understand why residents almost automatically accept their hurts as normal.

Demons don't play fair. They'll sneak back in on the elderly just as quickly as they afflict a small child who can't defend itself. So - illness does often reoccur. To help prevent this, we do teach residents how to refuse the unwanted spirits; some use the information, some don't.

Sometimes people are healed in a meeting where there may be a heavy anointing or presence of the Holy Spirit. Often, they may be healed primarily on someone else's faith. If they can read their Bible and get enough teaching, God expects them to defend themselves the second time around , should another attack occur.

We should add one common-sense caveat. The body of a born-again Christian is a temple of the Holy Spirit Who lives within the reborn spirit *(I Corinthians 6:19)*. So it behooves us to take care of our bodies. God expects it.

If the Lord heals someone of emphysema and that person continues to smoke, he's inviting the spirit of nicotine back and shouldn't count on being rehealed.

Pastor Tom tells about a young man in his church whom the Lord healed of near-deafness. The man had been listening to very loud MTV sounds. He was warned to stop it, but he didn't. Several times he lost his healing and several times a gracious God rehealed him. Still, he didn't get the message. Finally, as Pastor Tom relates, the young man couldn't get healed anymore. It was his decision to remain in the environment that produced his hearing loss.

We do have an uncommon health care Provider, but he does expect us to provide a certain amount of cooperation.

Clear the Air

"For our struggle is not against flesh and blood, but against the rulers, against the powers, against the world forces of this darkness"
(Ephesians 6:12)

Pat had problems in her office. People were nasty. There was backbiting, sniping and an abundance of swearing. Her work environment was polluted. Her mental well-being was threatened.

One evening, at a Bible meeting, Pat learned she could do something about the problem. Maybe she couldn't change the people involved, but God could move, when she did her part. She latched on to the promise of Jesus Christ that He had given her authority over all the power of the enemy (Luke 10:19), and that demons were subject to her. She knew , also, that whatever she bound on earth would be bound in heaven, according to Matthew 16:19 and 18:18.

Armed with her new knowledge and resolve, Pat began binding the spirits behind the acrid atmosphere in her office. In the name of Jesus, she bound criticism, backbiting, envy, lying, swearing and other people polluters. She did it daily, sometimes more often.

A few weeks later, back at the Bible meeting, Pat had a good report. In a week, the office atmosphere had changed dramatically. Workers were more pleasant. The contention and strife was less and so was the swearing. No longer did she go home with a headache. No more did she dread going to work. The Spirit of God had moved on the problem when she had done her part by binding the spirits involved in the name of Jesus according to the word of God.

And - since God doesn't play favorites (Acts 10:34) - you as a Christian and His child, can do the same with the same refreshing results.

As another example of how we can bind or refuse to permit evil spirits to operate on others around us, let's look at what Bud did.

One day, this local writer presented a massive, well-thought-out outline for a slide presentation for one of his clients., But, piece by piece, the client began picking the outline apart. The whole cloth of it was beginning to unravel.

That's when Bud began counter attacking. As he recalls, he began mentally (the client was too close to move his lips) rebuking the spirit of criticism in the name of Jesus, fast and furiously. After less than a minute, the client changed his attitude and said, "on the other hand" - and the outline was preserved. The critical spirit was rendered inoperative. The devil will come at us through other people, but, in the name of Jesus, we can stop him dead in his tracks.

Lucille's home could get very unpleasant when her husband came in from work. Cursing and vile language would flow out of his mouth. Lucille, aware of her preventive procedure, decided to improve that home environment. Just before her husband was due home, she began binding the spirit of cursing. And, the four-letter words stopped. Dinner was more digestible and so was conversation.

Pat, Bud and Lucille are only three examples of Christians moving into God's prevention mode. You can be another one. Why put up with demonic garbage? Don't let it unload on your turf! Remember that command - "Spirit of (whatever it is), I bind (or refuse) you in the name of Jesus!" Take as necessary - and begin breathing more comfortably!

Carry Portable Coverage

"And surely I am with you always"
(Matthew 28:20 NIV)

Did your alarm ever sound off in the morning and though you knew it was time to get up, you just lay there blanketed in a mild stupor?

That's happened to me and I used to lose valuable time as a result. To make it worse, I would get uptight as I rushed around to get going.

But, one morning, I tried something that worked. I rebuked a spirit of stupor in the name of Jesus, and my languor began to leave. I became more wide awake.

The Song of Solomon (2:15) tells us the little foxes can spoil the vine. And that big fox, the devil, can assign his little foxes to spoil your day. But you don't have to let him! Instead, use your authority to head his evil forces off at the pass.

How? Let's go through what could be a typical day in the life of a Christian who knows he's seated with Jesus in the spiritual world and doesn't have to get knocked around during that day. Consider the following fictitious scenario that could have happened.

Joe gets up more quickly and easily after rebuking stupor. But while he's shaving, he remembers an important meeting later that morning. As fear starts to edge in, he slams the door on it by refusing that spirit in the name of Jesus.

As he sits down to breakfast and the too-runny fried eggs his wife has prepared, he's about to comment. Fortunately, he knows Jesus said not to criticize, and in his mind he refuses a critical spirit. Keeping his mouth shut, he avoids Round One in what could have been an early morning argument.

After breakfast, Joe kisses his wife goodbye, telling her he loves her because he does and he also knows God's word says love never fails.

Crouched behind the wheel of his car in morning rush-hour traffic, he realizes he's getting uptight - and he rebukes a spirit of tension. His shoulders relax and he drives with more peace and less aggression. Resisting the temptation to ingest the bad news on the radio, he pops in a Bible tape and arrives at work more relaxed and more knowledgeable of the good news of Jesus Christ.

Joe is glad he saturated himself in the Bible, because when he walks into the office, the boss, who always manages to beat him in, lays into him unfairly for a mistake he didn't make. As Joe feels anger and resentment begin to arise, he resists those spirits and quickly forgives (in his mind) the boss. Eventually, the boss learns the truth - someone else, not Joe, made that mistake. Thinking back, he's amazed at the calm reaction of his unfairly accused employee. This guy is different, he decides, maybe I should give him more responsibility.

At his desk, preparing for the upcoming client meeting , Joe is distracted by a loud-mouth, foul-mouth who's spraying the air with unmentionable language. Knowing the poor guy doesn't know a spirit of swearing is using him, Joe, under his breath, starts binding a spirit of swearing, in the name of Jesus. After a few minutes, the cussing ceases.

On the elevator as he leaves for the meeting, our hero remarks about what a beautiful day it is. And even though other passengers look at him oddly - and one quickly comments "This can't last", Joe keeps smiling, knowing God's word tells him to think about the good things.

The business meeting is successful, in large part because Joe kept binding critical spirits on the client - and rebuked a spirit of anxiety that tried to get on him just before it was his turn to contribute to the sales presentation. The result - a more relaxed, confident presentation.

Going to lunch at a nearby restaurant, Joe gets so involved in discussing the meeting that he walks right into a passerby. Apologizing, he binds a spirit of anger on the other person.

Back at work in the office, Joe begins to sneeze. His nose starts running. Knowing the Bible promises no weapon formed against him will prosper, he immediately begins refusing a head cold , doing it, of course, in the name of Jesus. In minutes, his nasal passages dry up and the would-be cold is aborted.,

Toward the end of the work day, activity becomes hectic and Joe starts to get stressed out and begins to get a headache. Aware of the scripture that Jesus bore the punishment for his peace, he rejects a spirit of stress and the headache disappears along with the stress.

Driving home in his car, Joe feels somewhat drained. Rebuking a spirit of fatigue, he begins singing praise choruses to God amid the bumper-to-bumper traffic. By the time he arrives home to greet his family, he feels great, almost exhilirated. The joy of the Lord has been his strength.

At dinner, Joe discovers his young son was emotionally wounded because he was put down in school by an older boy. Hugging his son, he also commands a spirit of rejection to leave the boy, who says, "Hey, dad, I feel a lot better!"

After dinner, his wife has to attend a church meeting, leaving him alone to help with homework. Really unfair, he thinks, and begins to feel sorry for himself. But he doesn't let a spirit of self pity get a grasp on him, instead, he tells it to leave in the name of Jesus. It does, and Joe is able to wade into the help-with-homework routine without suffering the "poor me" syndrome.

In fact, homework and bedtimes go so smoothly, Joe has time to read his Bible in peace.

As he looks back on his day, he counts up all the blessing God has given him in the past sixteen hours. The promise that he would reign in life through Jesus Christ has again been fulfilled. And he's appreciative that the same Holy Spirit that raised Christ from the dead lives in him and that God made him a part of His Health Maintenance Organization.

As he drifts off to sleep, Joe thanks God that the exercise of his faith is the healthiest exercise of all.

22. INSURING A BETTER DAY (stay-at-home moms)

Smooth Out Rough Days

"The young lion and the serpent you will trample down."
(Psalm 91:13)

Here's another possible scenario. This time we'll put you, young mother, into it.

You're a master juggler, though, being human, you do sometimes drop the ball. Busy does it, with pre-school child, in-school child, preparing, chauffeuring, soothing, responding . You know the subject-to-change routine.

Lying in bed in the A.M. and just thinking about the activities ahead can make you tense before you've batted an eyelid. But knowing that doesn't have to be, you quickly refuse a spirit of tension in the name of Jesus.

But, you are tired, in part because little Billy woke up from a nightmare and you could hear him crying. (Your husband is a sound sleeper.) So you leaped out of bed to calm the storm. You wonder why you can't get a decent night's sleep when you really need it - your husband always seems to manage. And as more "let's feel sorry for me" thoughts start coming up, you realize self-pity is at your door, so you refuse it along with a spirit of resentment. As a result, you start your day in a better mood.

At breakfast, Billy, teased by his older sister, heaves his milk at her. Looking at both of them, anger starts rising, but you put it in its place in the name of Jesus and calmly start cleaning up the mess. You make each child apologize (and forgive) the other. And the atmosphere improves.

With daughter off to school and husband off to work, you grab a piece of paper and start planning the day. Aware of what you want to accomplish in a few hours, you start getting anxious. Recognizing your arch-enemy, you refuse a spirit of anxiety and the planning process proceeds with greater ease.

Just as you're preparing to go shopping, the phone rings. It's that nice neighbor who's retired and has lots of time on her hands. She starts criticizing various neighbors for their evident shortcomings.

At this point, you begin mentally rebuking her critical spirit. The blaming stops, but the conversation goes on. You look at your watch.

You were hoping to stop at the bread store as well as the supermarket and get back in time for lunch. However, your neighbor is asking for advice and you don't want to cut her off. So you refuse a spirit of impatience and in time graciously exit.

Right after school, your daughter has a ballet lesson, but, for some reason, your car wont start. Billy has wandered off into the neighborhood and the furnace man has arrived ahead of time. Rebuking a spirit of confusion, you somehow work things out. You even recall how to handle the gas pedal so the starter kicks in.

Hurrying to the ballet lesson, (you're now behind time), you're afraid the next light might turn red before you reach it. What can you do about it, anyway? Speed? So you refuse a spirit of fear and realize you can turn before the light and take an alternate route.

Back from the ballet session, your daughter tries to pirhouette on the front steps and lands on her right arm instead of her feet. Nothing seems to be broken, but your daughter is crying. That's when you immediately take authority in Jesus' name and start rebuking spirits of pain and inflammation. The crying stops, there is virtually no redness on the bare arm. Calmly you and the kids sail into the house.

But you forget to check the answering maching until an hour before dinner. Your husband has called and left a message. Since he and the boss were making a late call in the neighborhood, your husband has invited him home for dinner - that night.

Angry thoughts start surfacing, but you refuse them in the name of Jesus. You remember a nearby store has a superb take-out salad bar well as a delicious barbecue chicken.

The meal is a great success. You especially enjoy the after-dinner conversation because you've bound a spirit of nicotine and the boss didn't light a single cigaret.

Your husband is so pleased he invites you out to dinner the next night. The nice neighbor you didn't offend on the phone earlier is pleased to baby sit.

Looking back that night, you realize the day worked out pretty well. And you thank Jesus for clearing barriers when you spoke to them in His name.

Just Use Your Clout

" And He put all things in subjection under His (Jesus') feet"
(Ephesians 1:22)
"and raised us up with Him and seated us with Him"
(Ephesians 2:6)

I was about to pray for a nursing home resident who was suffering from pain. Then I realized that he was a Christian as much as I was and he could handle the situation himself. So I told the pain-stricken man just how to rebuke that spirit of pain in the name of Jesus. He did it - and to his surprise, there was much less pain.

In another nursing home, where we had been teaching a Christian's position of authority in Jesus Christ, one of the residents who came to the Bible studies told us what happened when he refused to put up with a physical attack.

The gentleman prayed against a stomach ailment that was bothering him. He had repeated the prayer (as he called it) sixty times. At exactly that point, the stomach discomfort left him. Most likely it was some type of flu. Most certainly it left when that baby Christian (who was physically going on the age of 70) used the name of Jesus. Incidentally, he reported that the previous time he had a similar problem, it took several days to get well.

Do-it-yourself loosing can sometimes be done in less time than it would take to call the doctor for a presciption for valium. One evening, Ned called for help. He wanted to know if there was a book available with prayers for anxiety and worry. His wife had left him many months earlier and the young man was very concerned about the separation.

I told him it wasn't a matter of prayer but of taking authority in the name of Jesus Christ. Ned was a brand new Christian with very, very little spiritual knowledge. But, he had as much authority as the greatest evangelist on the face of the earth.

He was told what to do and how to do it. For anxiety, Ned simply said something like "Spirit of anxiety, leave me in the name of Jesus." He reported feeling less anxious. Then he went after a spirit of fear. More results. He felt lighter, better. Not only had he never done anything like that before, but this new Christian is a very soft-spoken and almost timid man.

The entire process was very simple. No shouting was necessary, just quietly commanding. And as always, Jesus backed His word and His name. Total time involved for the actual loosing was less than two minutes.

If any Christian can do what these people have done, why aren't more Christians doing it?

Consider Gulliver of fiction and film fame. This adventurous seafaring man came, one night, to a place called Lilliput, inhabited by tiny people called Lilliputians.

Gulliver was a giant compared to the natives. But he made the mistake of lying down and sleeping when he arrived. When he woke up, he was fettered by almost innumerable strands wound about him by the tiny Lilliputians.

In somewhat the same way, perhaps, the Body of Christ on earth, God's HMO, has been shackled by its demonic enemies. Like Gulliver, its members have been taken prisoner by many strands - ignorance, religion, tradition, fear, doubt, you name it.

That, I believe, is changing, as more and more Christians are learning they are giants in Jesus, understanding their authority in Him, recognizing the devil's devices and rising up to shake them off.

This book, hopefully, will add to that acceleration of knowledge, faith and action. We pray that more people will walk in divine health - and be witnesses to a spiritually-hungering world of what it really means to be a follower of Jesus Christ.

Take This Prescription

*"that at the name of Jesus every knee should bow, of those
who are in heaven, and on earth, and under the earth"*
(Phlippians 2:10)

If you're a born-again Christian, here's what you do.

At the first or early signs of a mental or physical incursion, pull
out the key of **binding** (or refusing to permit). (See Chapter 5.) Remember, Proverbs 18:10 promises "The name of the Lord is a strong
tower; The righteous runs into it and is safe." Also recall that in
John 17:11 Jesus prayed we would be kept safe by the power of His
name.

Specifically , let's say you're starting to feel anxious. Simply "
speak to the mountain" as follows. "Spirit of anxiety, I refuse you in
the name of Jesus." If you like, you can add an appropriate scripture
such as Jesus' injunction not to be anxious , in Luke 12:22.
Perhaps fear is attacking. You say, "Spirit of fear, I refuse you in
the name of Jesus." Again, you can add an appropriate scripture such
as Psalm 118:6, "The Lord is on my side; I will not fear"(KJV). However, while including scriptures is helpful, it isn't necessary.
On the physical side, if you're getting a headache, here's the rem-
edy. Say to it, "Spirit of headache, I refuse you in the name of Jesus."
For a head cold, "Spirit of head cold, I refuse you in the name of
Jesus."

Whatever the symptoms: stress, tension, flu, queasiness, pain -
speak to the problem by name - refusing it in the name that is above
all names, the name of Jesus.
You may have to repeat the command more than once. Keep doing
it until the symptoms leave.

To stop a spirit attacking you through someone else, simply bind it
in the name of Jesus; ie - "Spirit of criticism, I bind you in the name
of Jesus." If the particular problem has been around awhile, and has

a hold on you, then you must **loose** it, from yourself, or from the person you're helping. Don't loose from a non-Christian. That person cannot use the authority of Jesus to prevent the spirit from returning and bringing others with it. *(Matthew 12:43-45)*

To loose, as with binding (or refusing), you speak to the specific mountain. If you're down with the flu, say "Spirit of influenza (or flu), get out in the name of Jesus." You do have the flu, but it has to go when you tell it to.

Maybe you've become depressed. Same principle, "Spirit of depression, get out in the name of Jesus."

And - in every case - speak as if you mean it. Jesus spoke with authority. His people should do the same.

Binding (or refusing) and loosing is not an exact science. I can't tell you how many times you'll have to speak to your mountain - once or much more. Also, as Chapter 7 covers, there may be blocking spirits that must be expelled first. If you're not sure what emotional or mental spirits may be blocking physical healing, pray to the Lord. He doesn't want you ignorant.

Often, as we point out in Chapter 13, a physical, mental or emotional spirit may be inherited. If that's the case, you speak to the inherited spirit: "Inherited spirit of (whatever), get out in the name of Jesus." If your sister, mother or grandparent had the problem, you may have "inherited" it from them.

Another possible blocker to healing is unforgiveness. If you're holding anything against someone - even if it is their fault - God says you must forgive *(Mark 11:25,26)*. Also, if you have any other unconfessed sin, confess it to God and get on with your deliverance process.

Sometimes, you're where you can't speak out loud. Don't worry. Speak in your mind. It will work. God is a deliverer, not a legalist.

And be aware, the same devil who would lay sickness , pain and harmful thoughts and emotions on us, may try to do the same after we've been freed. Be ready to refuse in the name of Jesus should this happen.

Finally, remember the words of I Peter 5:8, "Your adversary, the devil, prowls about like a roaring lion, seeking someone to devour.

But resist him, firm in your faith". When you do, the afflicter has to flee *(James 4:7)*. That's a key stipulation in God's Health Care Plan. Count on it - access the Plan and reap the benefits!

Contrast God's Benefits

"To whom then will you liken God?"

(Isaiah 40:18)

Admittedly, some groups and companies are very large and cover millions of people. Some government plans would be more expansive.

However, there is no other plan available that covers between five hundred million and one billion people. Now that is a group.

There is also no other health care insurer or provider that's been around as long as this One.

With other plans, there may be a deductible. The only deductible aspect of God's plan is that you can deduct and eliminate all kinds of sicknesses and diseases.

Compare the coverage. Most plans don't cover everything and for an unlimited time. Mental care is just one example. But, God's plan has no limits in coverage and the number of days you can receive benefits. It's as open-ended as they come.

Portability? At work or out of it, new employer or none, you're covered, no matter where you happen to be.

Age is no factor, either. You won't be cut off when you reach seventy or eighty. You won't have to switch to some high-risk, high-cost classification or company. Ever.

Don't be concerned with reading the small print. There isn't any - unless you're using a small-print Bible.

And in what other plan is the very finest physician, surgeon, chiropractor, psychiatrist and psychologist constantly available at no charge?

Remember house visits? They can be unlimited with this plan. Anytime you need help, you don't have to wait for office hours, either. God is always on call.

Cost comparisons are extremely eye-opening. With God's Health Care Plan, there are no premiums or fees.

Looking at the bigger picture, imagine how this country could reduce its humongous health care costs if you and enough others accessed this no-cost health care. Billions of dollars could be saved annually. Your taxes could go down, your disposable income could be less indisposed.

You should also know this Insurer doesn't mind if you remain in any other plan. And you can be sure your current insurerer won't mind paying fewer claims!

So why limit your coverage and care? If you're a born-again Christian, start enjoying the benefits of God's Health Care Plan. If you aren't a Christian, the next chapter will show you what to do.

Get Into the Plan Today

The one and only requirement for enrollment in this far superior health care plan is to be a born-again Christian. Jesus said in John 3:3, "Truly, truly I say to you, unless one is born again, he cannot see the kingdom of God." In John 3:7, He states, "You must be born again." Pretty hard to misinterpret that. And it's only citizens of the kingdom of God, and the church of Jesus Christ, that are entitled to health care coverage from this highly paternal and fraternal organization. If you were a Moose, would you expect to be insured by the Elks?

What is "born again", anyway? In that Third Chapter of John, Jesus points out there are two births, the physical and the spiritual. First, we are born physically, then we can be born again, spiritually. When that spiritual birth occurs, we become plugged into the atoning sacrifice of Jesus Christ, because we have just asked Him to be our Lord and Savior. Heaven becomes our destination and a better life on earth is also promised. In John 10:10, Jesus declares he came to give us life (eternal) and a more abundant life (temporal). The latter includes the right to healing and health, including the privilege of using His name against those forces that would harm us.

All it takes to become born again (or born from above) is to pray a simple prayer such as the following.

"Lord Jesus, I believe in my heart that God raised you from the dead. I ask you now to come into my heart and be my Lord and my Savior. And I say with my mouth, "Jesus Christ is my Lord." *(Romans 10:9, 10)*

Did you pray that? Welcome to the family of God! And know you're now enrolled in His unique Health Care Plan for all the members of His family. Every provision and benefit the Great Provider offers in the Bible can be yours.And that includes the right and privilege of using that wonderful and powerful name of Jesus Christ.

Access the plan now - and start walking in divine health and begin helping others do the same!

Spiritual Exercises

"So then faith comes by hearing, and hearing by the word of God."
(Romans 10:17 NKJV)

1. Exercise your faith and build your spiritual muscle

Speak aloud to yourself —

* I'm a child of God ..an heir of God and a fellow-heir with Christ. *(Romans 8:16, 17)*
* I'm seated with Jesus in the spirtual world, high above the devil and every demon. *(Ephesians 1:20-23 & Ephesians 2:4-6)*
* Jesus has given me authority to tread on the devil and every demon. *(Luke 10:17,19)*
* I'm a believer, therefore I shall cast out demons. *(Mark16:17)*
* Whatever I bind or refuse to permit on earth will be bound (not permitted) in heaven. Whatever I loose on earth will be loosed in heaven. *(Matthew 16:19 & 18:18)*
* I will resist the devil and he will flee from me. *(James 4:7)*
* I know Jesus will confirm His word for me. *(Mark 16:20)*

2. Exercise your authority

Pick, or insert, whatever may be pertinent at the first sign of difficulty. End every command " IN THE NAME OF JESUS."

* Spirit of pain,I refuse you.....
* Spirit of arthritis(or indigestion, headache, etc), I refuse you...
* Spirit of discouragement, I refuse you...
* Spirit of fear, I refuse you...
* Spirit of anxiety, I refuse you...
* Spirit of stress, I refuse you....
* Spirit of resentment, I refuse you...
* Spirit of anger, I refuse you...
* Spirit of rejection, I refuse you...

- Spirit of inadequacy, I refuse you...
- Spirit of lust, I refuse you....
  (anything else that attacks- refuse it!)

If the problem is already resident......"Spirit of (whatever) get out, in the name of Jesus."

Healthy Reading

Authority in Three Worlds . . . . Charles Capps
The Believer's Authority . . . . Kenneth Hagin
Christian, Set Yourself Free . . . . . Graham & Shirley Powell
Defeating Dark Angels . . . . Charles H. Kraft
Deliver Us From Evil . . . . Don Basham
Demons and Deliverance . . . . Frank Hammond
Demons the Answer Book . . . . Lester Sumrall
God Heals Today. . . . . Chuck Schiappacasse
Healing Handbook . . . . Charles & Frances Hunter
Healing Promises . . . . Kenneth & Gloria Copeland
How to Heal the Sick . . . . Charles & Frances Hunter
Jesus Taught Me to Cast Out Devils. . .Norvel Hayes
Medicine For the Mind. . . . . Steve Sampson
The Name of Jesus . . . . Kenneth Hagin
Pigs in the Parlor. . . . . Frank & Ida Mae Hammond
Released to Reign . . . . Charles Trombley
Spiritual Warfare . . . . Michael Harper
Victory in Spiritual Warfare . . . . . Gary Whetstone
You Can Hear the Voice of God . . . . .Steve Sampson

AFTERWORD

Are we guaranteeing you healing and health if you do what this book suggests and outlines? Of course not. But we have related what we've learned and personally experienced plus Biblical bases for health and healing in the name of Jesus Christ.

In the great majority of incidents related in the book, we've used pseudonyms. In this way, no one need be embarassed by anything we've related. However, we can assure you the healings/deliverances did occur. When first and last names are used, these are the actual names of the persons involved.

We Christians have a magnificent Father and a marvelous Savior. They want only the best for us. Our healing has been purchased by the blood and the wounds of Jesus Christ, the Son of God, God the Son.

How can we ignore so great a salvation?

INDEX

"For nothing will be impossible with God."

(Luke 1:37